Ralph Modder

THE
SINGAPORE
CHINESE
MASSACRE

18 February to 4 March 1942

Horizon Books
Singapore • Kuala Lumpur
www.horizonbooks.com.sg

First published in 2004 by

HORIZON BOOKS PTE LTD
Block 5 Ang Mo Kio Industrial Park 2A
#05-12/14 AMK Tech II
Singapore 567760
E-mail: horizon@horizonbooks.com.sg
www.horizonbooks.com.sg

HORIZON BOOKS SDN BHD
Wisma Yeoh Tiong Tee
72C Jalan Sungai Besi
57100 Kuala Lumpur
Malaysia
E-mail: horizon@wismaytt.com

Cover design: Cheryl Marie Song

Computer graphics (maps): Kemal Modder

Photography (Singapore): Ken Lim Hong Kwee

ISBN 981-05-0388-1

Dedication

This book is respectfully dedicated in memory of the many thousands of Chinese civilians who were executed by the Japanese Army in the *Sook Ching* Massacre following the surrender of Singapore by the British on 15 February 1942. It is also in memory of the many thousands who sacrificed their lives in the defence of Singapore and the appalling number who died as the result of brutal treatment by guards at prisoner-of-war and civilian internment camps in Singapore and elsewhere in Southeast Asia.

— THE PUBLISHERS.

About the Author

Ralph Modder is a veteran Singaporean writer and journalist who worked on newspapers and magazines in Singapore, Malaysia and Hong Kong. He was born in Chemor, Perak. At a young age he and his family came to live in Singapore where he was educated. He was in Singapore during the Japanese occupation from 1942 to 1945.

He wrote several screenplays and stories, including the 'classic' *Sergeant Hassan*, starring the legendary Malay film actor Tan Sri P. Ramlee. The film had a Royal Charity Premiere and was attended by the King and Queen of Malaysia. The premiere was in aid of families of soldiers of the Royal Malay Regiment who had died in battles during the Japanese invasion of Malaya and Singapore in 1941-42.

Other titles by the same author, published by Horizon Books:
Souls The Gods Had Forsaken
Curse Of The Pontianak

Contents

Author's Note   vii

Introduction   1
A Long Trail Of Blood and the
'Sook Ching' Massacre
Chapter 1   37
Grim Reminders Of War
Chapter 2   44
Uncertainty And Suspicion
Chapter 3   46
A New Terror
Chapter 4   51
Gen. Yamashita's Dilemma And The POW Problem
Chapter 5   56
War Criminals Are Charged
Chapter 6   59
The Massacre
Chapter 7   70
'Terrified People'
Chapter 8   74
The $50 Million 'Donation'

End Notes
Tsuji: 'Master-mind' Of The Massacre   78
Tojo's Plea Of Innocence   83
Bringing War Criminals To Trial   85
They Fought To The Last Man   87
'The Battle For Singapore'   89
The Day Singapore Surrendered   103
Kempeitai Torture/The 'Double Tenth Trial'   110
Chinese Evacuation   117
The 'Tiger Of Malaya' Surrenders   120
The Japanese Soldier   125
The Horror Of Nanking   130
Bibliography   134

Author's Note

In war, there are no victors; everyone is a loser.
—Neville Chamberlain, British Prime Minister 1937-1940

Thousands of innocent male Chinese civilians between the age of eighteen and fifty-five were massacred soon after the British had surrendered Singapore to Japanese forces on 15 February 1942.

Briefly, this is what happened:

On 18 February, on the orders of Lt.-Gen. Tomoyuki Yamashita, the victorious commander of the Japanese 25th Army, the *Kempeitai,* the dreaded Japanese military/secret police supported by detachments of troops known as *Hojo Kempeitai (*auxiliary *Kempeitai)* set up 'screening and registration' centres in Singapore on the pretext of discovering suspected 'anti-Japanese elements' among the Chinese population. The 'suspects' were selected at random and interrogated briefly, or not at all. Those selected for execution were roped together in groups and taken in convoys of trucks to isolated places, mostly beaches, where they were shot. The executions 'officially' ended two weeks later on 4 March, although arrests of 'suspects' by the *Kempeitai* continued.

Senior Japanese army officers had admitted at a War Crimes Trial in Singapore in 1947 that some 5,000 male 'anti-Japanese elements' were killed, although the number claimed to have been executed is said to be about 50,000. To this day the actual figure is unknown.

It was one of the worst atrocities by the Japanese army against Chinese civilians after the 'Rape Of Nanking' in 1937 when at least 260,000 people (according to official figures) including women, children and infants and some 40,000 surrendered Chinese troops were slaughtered in a bloodbath of rape and cruelty that had shocked the world.

This book is not intended to revive old hatreds and prejudices or to reopen emotional wounds that may have healed during the passage of time. It is intended to present the factual circumstances surrounding a terrible massacre that was the most gruesome and tragic episode of the Japanese Occupation of Singapore from 1942 up to the time of the surrender of Japan in 1945. Evidence of the executions was revealed during The Chinese Massacre Trial.

Mention is made of the political ideologies of the militarists in power in Tokyo before the invasion of China, the annexation of Manchuria in 1931 and preceding the outbreak of the Pacific War in 1941. It might help to understand the reasons for Japanese territorial expansionism and aggression based on the fanatical belief that they were a 'superior race with divine origins' and destined to rule the world.

Belief in their racial superiority had contributed largely to the inhumane treatment of many thousands of surrendered Chinese troops and civilians during the Sino-Japanese War as well as masses of people in territories in Southeast Asia occupied by their troops who were treated as 'inferior' human beings. Included in this category were Allied prisoners-of-war and civilian internees who suffered unspeakable torture and hardship as was revealed during the trials of Japanese war criminals.

The Japanese also suffered heavily in the war. The atomic-bombings by the US of Hiroshima and Nagasaki in August 1945 alone had caused some two hundred thousand civilian deaths.

Ralph Modder
April 2004

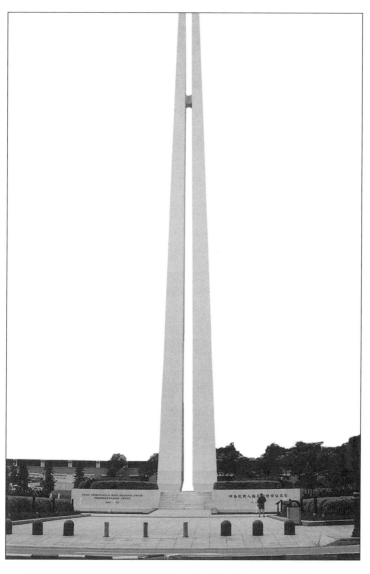

**MEMORIAL TO THE CIVILIAN VICTIMS
OF THE JAPANESE OCCUPATION,
AT RAFFLES CITY, 1942-1945**

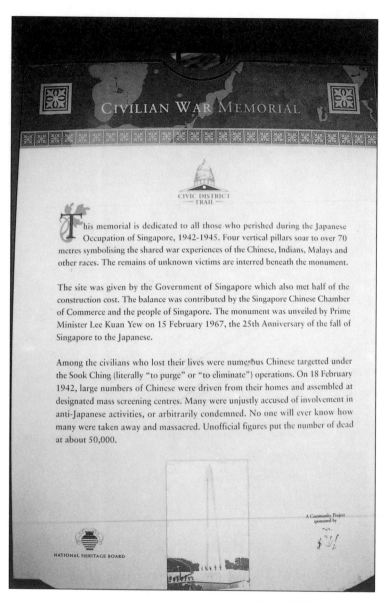

CIVILIAN WAR MEMORIAL

CIVIC DISTRICT TRAIL

This memorial is dedicated to all those who perished during the Japanese Occupation of Singapore, 1942-1945. Four vertical pillars soar to over 70 metres symbolising the shared war experiences of the Chinese, Indians, Malays and other races. The remains of unknown victims are interred beneath the monument.

The site was given by the Government of Singapore which also met half of the construction cost. The balance was contributed by the Singapore Chinese Chamber of Commerce and the people of Singapore. The monument was unveiled by Prime Minister Lee Kuan Yew on 15 February 1967, the 25th Anniversary of the fall of Singapore to the Japanese.

Among the civilians who lost their lives were numerous Chinese targetted under the Sook Ching (literally "to purge" or "to eliminate") operations. On 18 February 1942, large numbers of Chinese were driven from their homes and assembled at designated mass screening centres. Many were unjustly accused of involvement in anti-Japanese activities, or arbitrarily condemned. No one will ever know how many were taken away and massacred. Unofficial figures put the number of dead at about 50,000.

A Community Project sponsored by

NATIONAL HERITAGE BOARD

INSCRIPTION AT THE MEMORIAL
(see following page.)

The text of the inscription on the previous page reads:

This memorial is dedicated to all those who perished during the Japanese Occupation of Singapore, 1942-1945. Four vertical pillars soar to over 70 metres symbolizing the shared war experiences of the Chinese, Indians, Malays and other races. The remains of unknown victims are interred beneath the monument.

The site was given by the Government of Singapore which also met half of the construction cost. The balance was contributed by the Singapore Chinese Chamber of Commerce and the people of Singapore. The monument was unveiled by Prime Minister Lee Kuan Yew on 15 February 1967, 25th Anniversary of the fall of Singapore to the Japanese.

Among the civilians who lost their lives were numerous Chinese targeted under the Sook Ching (literally 'to purge' or 'to eliminate') operations. On 18 February 1942, large numbers of Chinese were driven from their homes and assembled at designated mass screening centres. Many were unjustly accused of involvement in anti-Japanese activities or arbitrarily condemned. No one will ever know how many were taken away and massacred. Unofficial figures put the number of dead at about 50,000.'

JAPANESE WAR MEMORIAL

A memorial at the Japanese Cemetery Park in Chuan Hoe Avenue off Yio Chu Kang Road, Singapore, in honour of some ten thousand Japanese soldiers who died during the invasion of Malaya and Singapore in 1941-42. Also buried at the cemetery are the remains of 135 Japanese war criminals who were executed at Changi Prison, Singapore. Many of them were convicted for their parts in The Singapore Chinese (Sook Ching) Massacre.

GRAVE OF JAPANESE COMMANDER

The grave of Field Marshal Count Terauchi (Commander, Japanese Southern Army) at the Japanese Cemetery Park, Singapore. Count Terauchi was the highest-ranking officer in the Japanese campaign in Southeast Asia. During the Japanese Occupation (1942-45) he resided at Government House (now the Istana and the official residence of Singapore's presidents). He was seriously ill at the time of the Japanese surrender in 1945 and was placed under house arrest by the British authorities in Johore Bahru. He died in early 1946. His ceremonial regalia was brought from Japan and buried with his remains.

Introduction

A Long Trail Of Blood
and the
'Sook Ching' Massacre

Among the appalling atrocities committed by the Japanese army in which huge numbers of Chinese civilians perished were: The Nanking Massacre ('The Rape Of Nanking') in December 1937 during the Sino-Japanese War and The Singapore Chinese Massacre (the *★Sook Ching* Massacre) in February-March 1942. Also, a series of massacres following the invasion of Malaya by Japanese forces in December 1941 at the start of the Pacific War.

The number of Chinese civilians massacred in peninsular Malaya is believed to be 100,000. More than 50 memorials were erected in their memory throughout the country. While Chinese and other communities in Malaya and Singapore suffered unspeakable tortures and death from disease and starvation during the Japanese Occupation, the Chinese being hated and despised 'historical' enemies of the Japanese also became the victims of mass executions. It was

Note: *★Sook Ching* is the Chinese translation of *shuku-sei* that in Japanese means, 'purification through purge.'

the repetition of a brutal policy against Chinese civilians by the Japanese army in China (following the annexation of Manchuria in 1931) in an all-out attempt to destroy the will of the Chinese people to resist Japanese domination of their country.

Civilians executed in Nanking during a six-week orgy of rape, indiscriminate slaughter and perverted cruelty that began on 13 December 1937 included people of all ages, students, women, children and infants. The International Military Tribunal of the Far East (IMTFE) sitting in Tokyo in 1946 estimated that at least 260,000 were killed. Other estimates had put the figure as high as 450,000 (see End Notes: *The Horror Of Nanking,* page 130).The world came to know of the carnage from reports and interviews with foreign businessmen, doctors, schoolteachers, missionaries and others who were in Nanking at the time.

Unlike the massacre at Nanking, there were no witnesses to The Singapore Chinese Massacre other than the Japanese troops who had machine-gunned, bayoneted or decapitated the victims mostly at lonely beaches, leaving the bodies to be carried away by the sea. The actual number executed was known only to high-ranking Japanese army officers and the *Kempeitai,* the dreaded secret/military police. They were among the 135 war criminals hanged at Changi Prison in Singapore, many for their parts in the massacre. They went to their deaths without divulging this information.

The survivors of four separate massacres gave evidence before a War Crimes Court in Singapore in 1947.They had escaped by pretending to be dead after being shot and wounded (see *The Massacre,* page 60) War Crimes investigators were convinced that a number of other mass executions had taken place besides those mentioned at the Massacre Trial.

However, due to the lack of evidence further action was not possible since witnesses or survivors had died during the Japanese Occupation.

At the end of the war in 1945, the Japanese War Office in Tokyo had vaguely admitted in a brief statement that 5,000 'anti-Japanese elements' among the Chinese community in Singapore were 'purged' in what they called 'The Singapore Incident.' The statement made shortly before the start of The Singapore Chinese Massacre Trial in March 1947, was seen as an attempt to belittle claims by the Chinese community that some 50,000 were executed. Many high-ranking Japanese officers were facing charges for their parts in the massacre and it was felt that such a claim might prejudice the outcome of their trials.

The mass executions took place following an order issued by Lt.-Gen. Tomoyuki Yamashita, commander of the victorious 25th Army immediately after the British had unconditionally surrendered Singapore on 15 February 1942. It called for all Chinese males between the age of eighteen and fifty-five to assemble at twenty-eight centres on 18 February for the purpose of being 'screened and registered.'

The ulterior purpose for this was to allow the *Kempeitai*, assisted by local informers, the chance to pick out members of Dalforce, (see End Notes: *They Fought To The Last Man,* page 87), a volunteer Chinese regiment that had fought courageously after Japanese troops had crossed the Straits of Johore and invaded Singapore on 8 February 1942. (The gallantry of the men of Dalforce would no doubt have reminded Japanese army commanders of the tenacious resistance by Chinese guerrilla-volunteers in the Sino-Japanese War.)

Gen. Yamashita had also wished to speedily eliminate any threat of organised anti-Japanese activity in Singapore that could jeopardise his plans for the imminent invasion of Sumatra and Java or threaten the lives of his troops stationed in Singapore for the purpose of keeping law and order.

A *Kempeitai* sergeant named Yamaguchi speaking in the Hokkien dialect explained to a crowd of Chinese in Nee Soon Village in Singapore why the *Sook Ching* 'screening and registration' operation was necessary. He said:

'While building a road if a tree is found to be causing an obstruction, not only is it cut down but its roots are also removed so that it could not grow again. The same would apply to a person who was guilty of a serious crime against the Japanese. Not only would he be removed, but also his "roots", meaning his family and close friends. By such action the population would be rid of dangerous elements. Our society would be purged and purified and become law-abiding and peaceful. So, you see, it is necessary to purify the population and to rid it of evil. The Japanese army was forced to carry out such purification methods in China against the enemies of Japan who had refused to co-operate with the Japanese authorities. If the Chinese people in Singapore also adopted this attitude, they too will be exterminated.'

Gen. Yamashita had divided Singapore into four sections, prior to the 'screening and registration' operation, each commanded by a general under his command:

Northern section: Lt.-Gen. Takuro Matsui, commander of the 5th Division.

Southern Section: Maj.-Gen. Saburo Kawamura, in charge of the Garrison Army and *Kempeitai* (Military Police). Eastern Section: Lt.-Gen. Takuma Nishimura, commander of the Imperial Guards Division.

Western Section: Lt.-Gen. Renya Mutaguchi, commander of the 18th Division.

Note: Gen. Kawamura was hanged for crimes committed during The Singapore Chinese Massacre. Gen. Nishimura was sentenced to life imprisonment for his part in the same massacre. He was also found guilty by a military court in Australia for having committed atrocities against wounded Australian and Indian troops during the fighting in Johore (Malaya) in January 1941. He was hanged. Gen. Mutaguchi was suspected of being involved in the massacre on 14 February 1942 of about 200 wounded British soldiers and staff at the Alexandra Military Hospital, Singapore He was not charged with any crime and was allowed to return to Japan.

From among the thousands assembled at the various 'screening and registration' centres, those to be executed were selected for bizarre reasons or for no reason at all. Many thought they had been singled out for the purpose of being issued with registration cards. Also selected were those with tattoos, English-speaking Chinese students and schoolteachers, employees of the British colonial government, civil defence workers, Chinese members of the Singapore Volunteer Corps (SVC) and supporters of the China Relief Fund.

More importantly, the executions would serve as a warning to the Chinese population of the brutal treatment they could expect should they refuse to cooperate fully with the Japanese. (It was an extension of the Japanese policy towards civilian populations in China: *Submit to Japanese rule or face extermination.*)

Also of serious concern to the Japanese was the communist-led Malayan Peoples Anti-Japanese Army

(MPAJA), comprised mostly of Chinese, operating in the jungles of Malaya and who had agents in Singapore.

Lt.-Col. Masanobu Tsuji (see End Notes: *Tsuji:'Master-mind' Of The Massacre,* page 78), who was Chief Planning Officer attached to Gen. Yamashita's 25th Army, had conceived a plan of revenge against the Chinese communities of Malaya and Singapore even before the Japanese invaded the two territories. This happened after he came into possession of   lists of names of prominent Chinese who were actively supporting the China Relief Fund in Malaya and Singapore and making large cash donations to the Nationalist government of China. The names were supplied to Tsuji by a network of Japanese spies operating in the two territories for a number of years before the Pacific War.

Tsuji's colleagues regarded him as a 'mystery man' and although a colonel, he was respected by officers of higher rank because they suspected him of being a spy for Japanese Prime Minister, General Hideki Tojo, to whom he secretly supplied information about senior officers of the 25th Army — including its commander Gen. Yamashita.

Tsuji's ulterior motive for the 'screening and registration' of Chinese following the surrender of Singapore was to discover members of the heroic Dalforce who were believed to be still at large. He had optimistically expected that 50,000 Chinese males would be executed during the five-day 'screening and registration' period originally planned from 18 to 23 February. However, he was to discover much to his anger that there was a 'lack of enthusiasm' among some army units in carrying out the executions, a reflection of his unpopularity among army commanders because of his arrogant attitude. He found he had no choice but to extend the operation until 4 March in the hope of achieving his 'target figure' or suffer a serious 'loss of face' and the trust of his powerful contacts in Tokyo.

Senior Japanese officers in their evidence at The Singapore Chinese Massacre Trial said they had 'been informed' that from 25,000 to 50,000 were executed.

Lt.-Col. Masayuki Oishi, head of No.2 Field *Kempeitai*, said in his evidence that shortly after the massacre began, Col. Tsuji had told him that 'the intention was to kill half the Chinese population of Singapore.' (The population of Singapore prior to the Pacific War was estimated at 500,000 of which some 400,000 were Chinese. This figure had doubled with the influx of Chinese refugees from Malaya following the Japanese invasion in December 1941.)

Tsuji returned to Tokyo after The Singapore Chinese Massacre. (Was it to receive the congratulations of Prime Minister Tojo for 'a job well done'?)

One of the surprises at the International Military Tribunal in Tokyo in 1946 was that Tojo, who was found guilty and hanged as a war criminal, had emphatically denied all knowledge of atrocities committed by Japanese forces anywhere during World War II. 'We did not even suspect that such things happened,' he had said (see End Notes: *Tojo's Plea Of Innocence,* page 83).

After the surrender of Japan, Col. Tsuji was reportedly in China where he was said to have been assisting US war crimes investigators. He was not prosecuted as a war criminal. Neither was he called to testify at The Singapore Chinese Massacre Trial.

The United States government after executing major war criminals in Tokyo had decided, for undisclosed reasons, not to investigate Tsuji and others suspected of war crimes.

Apparently, the British authorities in Singapore were in no position to reverse this decision. It was rumoured in

Singapore at the time that the US government had made a 'secret deal' with Tsuji, a mass murderer who had escaped the hangman because of his 'assistance' in certain 'classified matters'.

If there was a man who could have solved the mystery of the actual number of Chinese executed in The Singapore Chinese Massacre, it was Col. Tsuji. Or, would he too have taken the secret with him to the gallows at Changi Prison?

The US was more concerned with the economic rehabilitation of Japan and to remove the horrors of the atomic bombings of Hiroshima and Nagasaki in August 1945 that had hastened Japan's surrender. This was seen as necessary to secure Japanese support in the looming threat of World War III against the two communist 'giants', China and the Soviet Union.

However, it was felt in Singapore that the British government could not be excused for not bringing Tsuji back to face charges for the major part he had played in the Chinese Massacre. It was the British government's duty towards the families of the thousands of victims who had patiently awaited the defeat of Japan and for justice to take its course.

Anti-Japanese feelings among the Chinese community in Singapore had increased as the date for The Chinese Massacre Trial (10 March 1947) before a British War Crimes Court approached. In an obvious attempt to 'play down' its importance, *The Straits Times* that was British-owned at the time, published a comment by an anonymous War Crimes official a few days before the Massacre Trial began. He was quoted as saying that War Crimes investigators had estimated the total number of Chinese executed 'was about 5,000' and not 50,000 as claimed by some sources that probably included those Chinese who had died in Japanese air raids or in the intensified air and artillery bombardment in the weeks before the surrender of Singapore. (5,000 was mentioned by the Japanese War Office in Tokyo as the number executed in a report called 'The Singapore Incident'.) The newspaper report, however, failed to state how this figure came about since the remains of only an insignificant number of massacre victims were found buried in shallow graves in remote areas of Singapore.

Demonstrators outside the Victoria Memorial Hall where The Singapore Chinese Massacre Trial was being held included members of the Malayan Communist Party (MCP) whose militant arm, the Malayan Peoples Anti-Japanese Army (MPAJA), had conducted guerrilla warfare against the Japanese from the jungles of Malaya. Demands were made for the British authorities to publicly hang those Japanese sentenced to death for their parts in the massacre.

In speeches calling for 'revenge against the Japanese', the British authorities were criticised for their 'lack of interest' in the massacre and were reminded of the loyalty to Britain demonstrated by the Chinese communities in Malaya and Singapore who had made substantial donations to the British government at the start of World War II in 1939. They were also reminded of the gallantry of Dalforce during the Japanese invasion of Singapore in February 1942, when the volunteers had fought almost to the last man.

In the absence of proof to establish an 'official' figure of the number executed in The Singapore Chinese Massacre, the 'mythical' (5,000) figure supplied by the Japanese War Office in Tokyo was in due course accepted by the local and foreign media and war historians.

There were rumours of attempts being made in Tokyo and Singapore to conceal the actual number who were executed. It was felt that acceptance that the number of executions could be very much larger than what the Japanese War Office had disclosed would prejudice the trials of several senior Japanese army officers for their parts in the massacre.

Chinese community leaders in Singapore felt it would have been ludicrous to suggest that Col. Tsuji and the *Kempeitai* would have discontinued with the executions after 5,000 were killed, when there was no shortage of victims at 'screening and registration' centres. It would have been a severe 'loss of face' for Tsuji if he had accepted a greatly reduced number from the 50,000 'target figure' he had set out to achieve.

An 'Appeals Committee' was set up in Singapore to protest against some of the sentences handed down by the British War Crimes Court on Japanese officers found guilty for their parts in the massacre. However, such appeals ended abruptly since sentences imposed by military courts could not be the subjects of appeals in civil courts.

Evidence recorded during The Singapore Chinese Massacre Trial revealed that those who had been selected for execution at the 'screening and registration' centres were removed to secluded areas and roped together in groups. They were taken in convoys of lorries to remote beaches where they were lined up in small groups or as many as a hundred to two hundred at a time, and machine-gunned. Victims who were still alive were bayoneted to death by Japanese guards.

The bodies were carried away by the sea, a reason why beaches were more favoured as places for executions, although a few took place at rubber plantations where the bodies of victims were buried in shallow graves.

After each execution, the convoys of lorries returned to the 'screening and registration' centres to pick up more victims. This went on throughout the day and night for two weeks.

For some time after the massacre ended, large numbers of bodies of victims were found scattered on the beaches of the neighbouring Riau islands, along the coast of south Johore and islands in the South China Sea off the east coast of the Malaya.

The appalling atrocities by the Japanese army as revealed in evidence at War Crimes Courts in Southeast Asia, and International War Crimes Tribunals in Australia and Japan after the war had shocked the world.

Numerous Japanese suspected of committing atrocities had escaped prosecution and punishment because of the lack of evidence against them. Ironically, they had the British and American systems of justice to thank for their freedom and the fundamental point of any criminal proceedings:'that a person accused of a crime is innocent until proven guilty beyond all reasonable doubt.' Defence lawyers from the Supreme Court in Tokyo were provided those Japanese accused of serious war crimes that were punishable with death or life imprisonment. It was a far cry from the barbaric 'justice' administered by the Japanese during their occupation of Singapore and other territories that had resulted in the torture and deaths of many thousands of innocent people.

A reason offered by most of the Japanese on trial for their parts in The Singapore Chinese Massacre was that 'as soldiers they had no choice but to obey the orders of their superior officers.'

The fiery anti-Japanese sentiments of the overseas (Nanyang) Chinese and their overwhelming support for the Nationalist (Kuomintang) government that had been resisting the Japanese invasion of China since 1931, had no doubt contributed largely to their brutal treatment by the Japanese.

> **Note**: Prior to the Sino-Japanese War of 1937, a bitter conflict was fought between China and Japan in 1894–95 over territory in Korea in which China's navy was totally destroyed and its army routed by the Japanese. Formosa (Taiwan) was ceded to Japan from 1895 up to the time of Japan's surrender in 1945.

Chinese communities in Southeast Asia had contributed generously to organizations such as the China Relief Fund and gave their full support to the Western colonial governments in countries of their adoption that were being threatened by Japanese invasion.

For a number of years after the Japanese annexation of Manchuria in 1931, the large Chinese communities in Malaya and Singapore had organised boycotts of Japanese goods, the unloading of Japanese cargo ships as well as public anti-Japanese demonstrations. In addition, there was a steady stream of young Chinese men and women volunteers leaving Singapore and Malaya for China to join the Nationalist Army. The Japanese had further reason to be incensed with the Chinese in Malaya and Singapore because of the communist-led Malayan People's Anti-Japanese Army (MPAJA) based in the Malayan jungles.

It might have seemed to the Japanese after their occupation of Singapore, that while the 'British enemy' of some 130,000 troops and 4,000 civilians were in prisoner-of-war camps, the 'Chinese enemy' was still at large — and posing a serious threat to Japanese life and property.

A Japanese spy network in territories under Western

colonial rule in the Far East and Southeast Asia had been sending important military intelligence to Tokyo strategists for many years before the Pacific War.

It was revealed after the surrender of Japan that detailed information of 'secret' British fortifications in Hong Kong and the New Territories bordering China were in the hands of Japanese army commanders some months before the invasion began on 8 December 1941. (It took the Japanese army only seventeen days to wipe out British resistance in Hong Kong).

The Japanese were also in possession of details of all British defences in Malaya and the 'impregnable fortress', Singapore. (Malaya and Singapore fell to the Japanese in only seventy days.)

After the surrender of Singapore, such was the eagerness of the Japanese to take revenge on the 'Chinese enemy' that even before the 'screening and registration' of Chinese could officially begin on 18 February 1942, the *Kempeitai* had already begun executing groups of 'anti-Japanese' Chinese civilians in various parts of the island.

★ ★ ★

China, isolated from the rest of the world by feudal 'traditions' and harassed by clashes between rival warlords and betrayals by corrupt civil and military officials, became an unwilling 'guinea pig' for Japanese experiments at colonisation. These were conducted under the supervision of ruthless men in Tokyo who believed they were the direct descendants of the gods who had created the sacred islands of Japan.

The Japanese were ever mindful that the experience they gained in China as 'colonisers' would be put to good use in future encounters with the 'Chinese enemy' in Southeast Asia.

A senior Japanese army officer commented in Singapore after the surrender of Japan in 1945:'The Japanese hated and despised the Chinese more than they did the Americans and British. This feeling originated a long time ago and became something like an incurable disease.'

Before the grim details of The Singapore Chinese Massacre are presented, it is necessary to mention two 'acts of war against the Japanese army in China' for which Chinese troops were blamed. These 'incidents', as the Japanese called them, had led to hostilities and the horrific tortures and deaths of many thousands of innocent people, including women and children in villages, towns and cities in China.

The 'Mukden Incident' in 1931 resulted in the establishment of the state of Manchukuo (formerly Manchuria) with Pui-yi, the last emperor of China, as head of the puppet government.

'The Marco Polo Bridge Incident' in Peiping (Beijing) in 1937 resulted in a full-scale war between Japan and China.

Manchuria was to be only the beginning of an ambitious campaign for the whole of China to become subservient to Japan. Once this was accomplished, an all-out war would be launched for the establishment of a 'Greater East Asia Co-Prosperity Sphere.'

Western colonial possessions to be attacked would be: Indo-China, comprising Vietnam, Cambodia and Laos (administered by France) followed by British-administered Malaya, Singapore, Sarawak, Borneo, Brunei and Burma; the Philippines (administered by the United States); the Dutch East Indies (Sumatra, Java and some 13,000 islands of the Indonesian Archipelago, administered by the Netherlands);

also, New Guinea and some strategic islands in the central and south Pacific. India would be 'persuaded to join the 'Co-Prosperity Sphere' while Australia and New Zealand would be 'annexed'.

That, briefly, was the plan for the control of a vast area of immense natural resources that awaited the warlords in Tokyo who might have been forgiven for their growing impatience to get their hands on such fabulous wealth.

But, first the 'China Problem' had to be solved quickly and efficiently. To do so would require cunning and brazen treachery and military force even to the extent of exterminating large numbers of civilians. Such a plan would establish full Japanese sovereignty over Manchuria.

The Japanese had made one-sided treaties with China that were concluded with the familiar touch of blackmail and intimidation, resulting in Manchuria becoming a 'leased territory' of Japan's even before 'The Mukden Incident'.

Through the South Manchurian Railway that they owned, the Japanese controlled several towns and large cities such as Mukden; schools and public utilities, also the Kwantung Army, police and railway guards. Not content with having such a free hand, the Japanese took unfair advantage of concessions allowed them that resulted in frequent disputes with the Chinese authorities.

It had become obvious the Japanese were aggravating the situation on purpose. The only solution appeared to be the use of armed force that was favoured by powerful political factions in Tokyo such as the Black Dragon Society and the Cherry Society and extremists who demanded the recognition of Japan as 'the leader of Asia'.

There was some opposition by moderate political parties to such an aggressive policy and who favoured a 'friendly approach' in Sino-Japanese relations. These were rejected by supporters of the Cherry Society who strongly proposed that the army took action in settling the 'Manchurian Problem' and whatever future problems that might confront the Japanese in China.

Manchuria was regarded as Japan's 'life-line' in China over which it must have total and absolute control.

A period of political turmoil, assassinations and changes of government in Tokyo followed from which the Cherry Society emerged with a solution to the 'Manchurian Problem' that contained all the ingredients of a sinister, spine-chilling Hollywood action-thriller.

The main theme of this scenario was that any person or organisation suspected of being the enemy of the Japanese army would be also be considered an enemy of the Emperor. The penalty for such an offence was death.

The necessity to combine politics, economics, culture, national defence, etc. into a single unit under the Emperor was continually emphasised. There would be a 'single-mindedness' demonstrated by the Japanese people when it came to matters concerning national identity and the future well being and security of the nation.

The army was soon in a position to use its new powers to great advantage in the Cabinet and Diet, even ignoring opinions from the Emperor's advisers.

It was clear the Emperor had become a puppet of the powerful army clique that was making use of everything they could in their favour. It included two principles of Japanese ethical conduct that originated during the time of the founding of the Japanese Empire more than 2600 years ago. These were *hakko-ichiu* (the world as one united family) and *kodo* (total loyalty to the Emperor). They were repeatedly misinterpreted by the pro-army factions to suit the reasons for Japan's military aggression that was described as 'being in conformity with national policy' and suggested it had the Emperor's approval.

Nothing was further from the truth.

The Singapore Chinese Massacre was part of a notorious series of hostile action and atrocities that the warlords in Tokyo chose to describe as 'incidents'.

The Japanese invasion of China was known as 'The China Incident' that incorporated 'The Mukden Incident' and 'The Marco Polo Bridge Incident'. The massacre in Nanking was another 'incident'.

Nationalist Chinese troops were known as 'bandits' by the Japanese and not as soldiers. This was done in the hope that Japan would escape condemnation for numerous violations of international law in China as laid down by the Geneva Convention after World War I (1914-1918) and by the League of Nations, especially those concerning the humane treatment of people in occupied territories and prisoners of war.

Captured or surrendered Chinese troops were buried alive, shot, beheaded, bayoneted or sent to slave labour camps where they eventually died of torture and starvation.

It was clear to see that from the 'Mukden Incident' in Manchuria, the aim of the Japanese army was to conduct a campaign in China with such barbarity that the will, resilience and courage the Chinese people would finally be broken. Those who did not appreciate Japan's 'noble intentions' would be exterminated.

Extermination of 'the Chinese enemy' was seen by the Japanese as a 'military necessity' if total victory was to be achieved in China. In other words, the Chinese were presented with a choice: Either accept Japanese rule or be wiped out.

There was no doubt whatsoever that the Japanese were

determined to carry out their plan of extermination as seen in some northern areas, as well as in Shanghai, Nanking and elsewhere.

Faced with this prospect, the two main opposing political factions in China, the Nationalists and Communists, decided to temporarily bury their differences and combine to resist the Japanese. A similar 'unification policy' was adopted by the two rivals in Southeast Asia that added more clout to on-going anti-Japanese campaigns.

Pro-army and ultra-nationalist propagandists in Tokyo at the same time had stepped up their condemnation of the Chinese as 'a backward, corrupt and loathsome race for opposing Japanese leadership in China' and for not welcoming the Japanese who were 'divinely created to lead the world'.

While the Japanese army continued with mass executions of civilians in China, the air force carried out 'terror raids' on large Chinese towns and cities, resulting in heavy civilian casualties.

> **Note**: 'Terror air raids' were also carried out when the Japanese attacked Malaya and Singapore in 1941. The selected targets were Chinese-populated areas in Penang, Ipoh and Kuala Lumpur. In Singapore, casualties from air raids were the highest in Chinatown, a regular target for Japanese bombers. In the first air raid on Singapore in the early hours of 8 December 1941, 61 people were killed and 133 injured mostly in the Chinatown area.

THE JAPANESE INVASION OF CHINA

RUSSIA

SAKHALIN

Vladivostok

MANCHUKUO
(MANCHURIA)
Annexed 1931

Mukden

KOREA
(Annexed 1910)

Seoul

JAPAN

Tokyo

Osaka

Nagasaki

Beijing
(Peiping)

Nanking
("Nanking
Massacre"
Dec. 1937)

Shanghai

Hankow

CHINA

Chungking

CANTON

TAIWAN
(Formosa)
Annexed 1895

Okinawa

HONG KONG
(Invaded 8 Dec. 1941)

Hanoi

BURMA

'The Chinese Enemy'

What had motivated the Japanese to commit acts of such barbarity against the Chinese?

Western authors had pointed out that brutality was common in the Japanese armed forces. Punishments were 'gratefully accepted' by those who were punished as 'demonstrations of affection' by those of senior rank, and not as 'punishments' in the real sense of the word. It also demonstrated the total acceptance of 'superiority' over 'inferiority' (see End Notes: *The Japanese Soldier,* page 125).

To see a Japanese army private, his face streaming with blood, being slapped and punched by a corporal or a sergeant for some mistake he had made was not an uncommon sight during the Japanese Occupation of Singapore. Or, to see a sergeant being beaten by an officer or and an officer having his face slapped by someone of higher rank.

The only time when a private soldier could punish others was when dealing with 'inferior' enemy soldiers and civilians in China and in other Japanese-occupied territories.

A Japanese soldier who took part in the Nanking Massacre when asked by an American journalist at the end of World War II whether he had felt any compassion for those who were slaughtered, he replied:

'I was a young soldier when our troops occupied Nanking. Our officers told us we could kill and rape as many of "the Chinese enemy" as we pleased. There were some of us, however, who did not like the idea, including myself. When we did not join the others in shooting and bayoneting civilians, we were ridiculed and made fun of. Our troops were holding competitions among themselves to see who could shoot or bayonet to death the most Chinese within a specified time. Eventually, I was persuaded to join them. A sergeant told me with a laugh, "Killing a Chinese is just like killing a dog! You'll feel nothing! Try it and you'll see!" My first victim was an old Chinese woman. I aimed my rifle at her head. I pressed the trigger. I saw her brains spatter on the brick wall behind her. The other soldiers cheered and encouraged me. After that I killed many Chinese of all ages, even children. I did not feel any remorse. I also raped young girls before killing them. I became involved in the frenzy of killing and everything else that was going on. Later, I felt disgusted and horrified at what my comrades and I did. Others who were with me at the time felt the same way. I now spend my days praying for forgiveness.'

'The Mukden Incident'

A surprising shift in Japan's aggressive attitude towards China was seen with the announcement from Tokyo that a meeting between Foreign Minister Shigemitsu of Japan and Marshal Chang Hsueh-liang, the Finance Minister of China, would take place in Mukden on 20 September 1931. Its purpose was 'to settle all outstanding differences between the two countries'.

However, the much-publicised meeting was never held because on the night of 18 September the 'Mukden Incident', a treacherous plot hatched by senior officers of the Kwantung Army in Manchuria and the pro-army Cherry Society in Tokyo, was to shock the world.

Briefly, this is what happened:

At about 9pm on the night of 18 September, a young Chinese army officer belonging to the 7th Chinese Brigade and stationed at Mukden Barracks, reported to his superior officer that a train consisting of four coaches and an unusual-looking locomotive had halted on the railway line opposite the barracks. One hour later a loud explosion was heard followed by the sound of rifle fire.

According to the Japanese version of what happened (which was later discovered to be completely untrue) a Japanese army unit was on night patrol duty along the railway track when there was an explosion some two hundred yards away. Upon investigation the Japanese discovered that a section of the railway line had been blown up. The Japanese patrol was then fired upon. Japanese army reinforcements arrived on the scene and attacked the Chinese army barracks with rifle, machine-gun and artillery fire. Most of the Chinese soldiers escaped. However, the Japanese claimed that they had killed a few hundred Chinese troops. A report was also received that a Japanese regiment had attacked the walled city of Mukden. The following morning, Mukden's weapons depot and an airfield were in Japanese hands.

Japanese troops had used heavy artillery in the operation. Later, Colonel Seshiro Itagaki, the Japanese officer in charge of operations, admitted he had known about the attack a week before it took place and had secretly installed the artillery in readiness.

> **Note:** Col. Itagaki, was a prominent member of the notorious Kwantung Army clique based in Manchuria that advocated the total Japanese occupation of China, a policy that was strongly supported by the pro-military Cherry Society in Tokyo that also advocated the code of *kodo* (total loyalty to the Emperor). Itagaki was later promoted to lieutenant-general and was War Minister in 1938, during which time Japanese military aggression in China was intensified. He was recalled to the army before the outbreak of the World War II. He surrendered Japanese forces stationed in Singapore, Borneo and Sarawak to Lord Louis Mountbatten, commander-in-chief Allied Forces, in a ceremony at

the Municipal Building (now City Hall) in Singapore on 12 September 1945. He was found guilty by an International Military Tribunal in Tokyo in 1946 on charges of severely restricting food and essential medical supplies to prisoner-of-war and civilian internee camps under his charge, resulting in the deaths of thousands of prisoners from malnutrition and disease. Gen. Itagaki was hanged.

Meanwhile, the Japanese consul-general at Mukden was asked by the Chinese authorities to intervene in a bid to avert a serious clash in which Chinese troops would have been no match for the well-armed Japanese. Efforts by the consul-general failed to pacify the irate Col. Itagaki who was determined to continue with military action. Frantic efforts by Marshal Chang Hsueh-Liang for an end to the tense situation were also unsuccessful. The consul-general then made a final attempt to end the confrontation. He had explained in an urgent cable to the Foreign Ministry in Tokyo the serious nature of the situation and that the Chinese were doing everything they could to settle the matter in a peaceful way while Col. Itagaki insisted that 'since the matter concerned the prestige of the Japanese government and the army, military action must continue'. The consul-general's appeal was ignored by Tokyo.

There was no doubt the 'Mukden Incident' was provoked with the consent of high-ranking army officers and the sinister Cherry Society in Tokyo as well as by senior officers of the Kwantung Army to gain full control of Manchuria that would lead to the setting up of a puppet state (Manchukuo).

Several Japanese army officers who were implicated in the Mukden conspiracy were charged as war criminals before an International War Crimes Tribunal in Tokyo in 1948. They maintained that the action taken by the Kwantung Army was a 'reprisal' against a 'superior Chinese force' that had made a 'surprise attack' on Japanese army units who had later 'staged a counter-attack' and captured the city.

The truth is that Japanese troops were never attacked. It was the Chinese troops who were taken by complete surprise since they were unarmed and inside their barracks with all the electric lights switched on.

As stated at the Military Tribunal in Tokyo, the Japanese army had later achieved its objective of seizing Manchuria and by doing so had proved it was more powerful than the government in power and would not tolerate any opposition.

Encouraged by the success of the Kwantung Army, pro-army factions in Tokyo were prepared to adopt ruthless measures to wipe out any opposition to their future plans in China. Kidnappings and assassinations became highlights of the Japanese political scene and served as a warning to those who might oppose the army clique.

Japan's preparations for military aggression to establish itself as a 'master race' in control of Asia began many years before the Pacific War.

At the end of World War I in 1918, Japan was granted a mandate from the League of Nations for three groups of islands in the Pacific. These were the Mariana Islands, the Marshall Islands and the Caroline Islands. In disregard of the terms of the mandate that forbade the building of military installations, Japan secretly constructed fortifications on the islands. By 1935 a naval air base had been completed on the island of Saipan in the Marianas that was only two hundred miles from the US island of Guam.

A network of Japanese commercial enterprises in

territories administered by Western colonialists in Southeast Asia became the 'fronts' for espionage agents who supplied Tokyo with important military intelligence.

A famous spy in Singapore was S. Nakajima, a photographer who for many years had a studio at the Raffles Hotel Arcade. He was a popular figure and 'specialised' in taking photographs at official ceremonies and celebrations at the various British army establishments and air bases, and in particular the giant naval base at Seletar. On display in the 'window' of his studio were portraits of some high-ranking British commanders. Nakajima 'disappeared' from Singapore shortly before the outbreak of the Pacific War. It was only discovered after the surrender of Japan that he was an agent attached to Naval Intelligence Headquarters in Tokyo.

In Singapore 'fronts' for spies included the offices of Japanese consular and trade representatives, medical centres, massage parlours, *geisha* houses, brothels and restaurants. The build-up of information was eagerly received in Tokyo as pro-army factions prepared for the day when Japan would go to war against the 'Western imperialists'.

On the domestic front in Japan, emphasis was being placed on the education of youths with totalitarianism and world domination as the main themes. References were made in school textbooks to the Japanese as a 'divinely-created master race' and of Japan's 'noble mission' to end Western colonialism and the 'liberation of East Asia'.

Military strategists had pointed out that the presence of the British and American navies in the Pacific and Far East areas were 'hindering the realisation of Japan's peaceful objectives in East Asia'. This threat could only be removed by the creation of an 'invincible Japanese air force'. Such a theory was vividly put into action in the attack by carrier-based planes on Pearl Harbour on 7 December 1941

(Hawaiian Time) that crippled the US Pacific Fleet and the sinking of the battleship *Prince of Wales* and the battle-cruiser *Repulse*, Britain's main naval strength in the Far East, three days later on 10 December off the south-east coast of Malaya. The attack on the British warships was carried out by Japanese torpedo-bombers based in Saigon (Ho Chi Minh City).

By 1937 Japan was fully committed to the conquest of China. General Hideki Tojo, who later became wartime prime minister, was then a major-general in the Kwantung Army. He was confident of victory. But, he had not considered the amount of commitment by the Japanese army such a victory would take to achieve.

After the annexation of Manchuria, the campaign in China appeared far from over while Tokyo was still obliged to continue with preparations for the 'war of liberation' against the Western colonial powers in East and Southeast Asia.

In a series of diplomatic moves, the Japanese were able to convince Nazi Germany of their 'impending' conquest of China and after Japan had invited German economic participation in the 'new China', Adolf Hitler announced the recognition of the 'state of Manchukuo'.

A period of closer ties between Nazi Germany and Japan culminated with Japan joining the European 'Axis Powers' (Germany and Italy) in 1940.

It would have been interesting to have seen how Adolf Hitler and General Tojo, both claiming to be the leaders of 'master races' and with similar plans for 'new world orders' would have compromised had the 'Axis Powers' become victorious in World War II.

(A Japanese interpreter at the War Crimes Trials in

Singapore in 1947 when asked this question by a British news agency representative, may have supplied the correct answer when he said: 'There would never have been a compromise between the two powers, one from the East and the other from the West. It would have been like trying to mix oil and water. Japan would have attacked Germany in an all-out attempt to rule the world!')

Immediately after joining the 'Axis Powers', Japan began to speed up plans to attack British, American, French and Dutch possessions in Southeast Asia.

Training for the attack on the US naval base at Pearl Harbour and practice landings by Japanese troops on the beaches of Hainan Island and along the coast of China had been completed in preparation for the landings scheduled to take place at Kota Bahru in the state of Kelantan on the north-east coast of Malaya, Patani and Singora on the south-eastern coast of Siam (Thailand) to the north of Kota Bahru. With General Tojo in firm control of the government and the Emperor, all obstacles to the army's plans for action were removed.

The stage was now set for war and the establishment of a 'Greater East Asia Co-Prosperity Sphere', a Japanese 'dream' that became a horrible nightmare for millions of people from China to Southeast Asia.

The International Military Tribunal (Far East) in Tokyo in its judgment delivered in 1948 on 'Japanese aggression', said: 'During the period of several months the Tribunal had heard evidence from a large number of witnesses who testified in detail to atrocities committed in all theatres of war on a scale so vast, yet following so common a pattern, that only one conclusion is possible. The atrocities were either secretly ordered, or willfully permitted by the Japanese government or individual members thereof, and by leaders of the armed forces.'

> **Note:** The League of Nations was the first international organization of nations. It was formed in Geneva in 1920 after World War I (1914-1918). Its role was to resolve conflicts peacefully and avert another war. The League did not have much influence. As an example of its weakness, it was only able to protest against the Japanese invasion of Manchuria in 1931 and took no further action. After World War II it was replaced by the United Nations.

'The Marco Polo Bridge Incident'

On the night of 7 July 1937 an officer in charge of a unit of Japanese troops who was engaged in 'manoeuvres' near the Marco Polo Bridge at the junction of the Peiping (now Beijing), Tientsin and the Peiping-Hankow railway in north China, reported that his men had been attacked by Chinese troops. Using this as a pretext, Japanese army commanders were quick to order full-scale attacks on surrounding Chinese provinces. The Japanese army went on the rampage. Cities defended by the poorly-equipped troops of General Chiang Kai-shek, the Nationalist leader, were no match for the Japanese who had modern weapons; the result of Japan's secret 'modernisation' campaign for its armed forces.

The important cities of Tientsin, Peiping and later Shanghai and Hankow fell to the Japanese as did the port city of Canton. The next to be attacked was the great city of Nanking, the headquarters of General Chiang Kai-shek's government from which his troops had now withdrawn.

The League of Nations was powerless to halt the increasing number of atrocities by Japanese troops against

Chinese civilians. Also targeted by the Japanese were American residents in China. American schools and hospitals were bombed and there were attacks on American boats patrolling the Yangtze River to protect the lives of American nationals. These attacks were in response to increasing US pressure on Japan to halt its aggression in China and to withdraw its troops.

The Japanese response was that the Mukden and Marco Polo Bridge 'incidents' were 'internal affairs between China and Japan' and was of no concern to 'outsiders'.

In June 1938, Cordell Hull the US Secretary of State, strongly condemned the sudden increase in the number of indiscriminate bombings of Chinese civilians by the Japanese air force. As the death toll of civilians killed in air raids steadily mounted, Japanese stocks of oil, all of which were imported, were being severely affected. However, US oil shipments to Japan continued because the US government wished to abide by an oil agreement.

US ambassador to Japan, Joseph C. Grew, warned that if US oil supplies to Japan were stopped, it could force the Japanese to go to war and move their forces south towards the oil-rich territories of Sumatra and Borneo. Grew argued that neither an oil embargo nor any other economic sanctions should be imposed on Japan 'unless the US was prepared to see them through to their logical conclusion, that might mean war'.

It was not until July 1941 that President Roosevelt issued an order freezing Japanese assets in the United States and the suspension of oil exports to Japan.

Prince Fumimaro Konoye (the elite Konoye Imperial Guard Division was part of the 25th Army that captured Malaya and Singapore in 1941–42 and took part in The Singapore Chinese Massacre) who was a former prime minister, declared in December 1938 that Japan would consider ending the Sino-Japanese conflict if China accepted the 'independence' of Manchukuo (Manchuria), submitted to Japanese military occupation and agreed to the establishment of an 'economic zone' controlled by Japan.

These proposals were rejected by the US.

The following year Japan made approaches to the two members of the 'European Axis Powers', Nazi Germany under Adolf Hitler and Italy under Benito Mussolini, with a view to a forming a military and political alliance. This was seen as a precautionary measure in the event of either side becoming involved in a conflict with the Soviet Union.

Early in 1939 Japanese troops invaded the strategic island of Hainan that lies just north of Vietnam in the South China Sea. The island would provide a valuable 'springboard' for a landing by Japanese troops on the east coast of Siam (Thailand) and Malaya should war break out between Japan, the United States and Britain.

Japanese strategists made another significant move by sending troops to occupy the Spratly Islands off Vietnam. It added support to the suspicion that Japan was getting very close to invading Southeast Asia.

As Hitler's armies swept through Europe, the Japanese stepped up their propaganda from Radio Tokyo about 'liberating' colonies controlled by 'evil Western powers' and the establishment of a Greater East Asia Co-Prosperity Sphere.

In August 1940, the puppet Vichy government in German-occupied France 'permitted' the Japanese to occupy Indochina and to construct airbases in the north. One month later, Japan officially joined the Axis Powers. Expected political 'back-scratching' followed with Japan recognising the 'New Order In Europe' and Germany and Italy recognising Japan's 'New Order In Greater East Asia'. The mutual recognition of the 'New Orders' on both sides of the world added further concern to Japan's intention to invade Southeast Asia.

The Tokyo warlords were confident that Germany would come to Japan's aid in the event of war with the United States. But, the bonds of the new 'brotherhood' between Germany and Japan were loosened after Germany invaded the Soviet Union in June 1941.

Adolf Hitler, the German *fuehrer* had fully expected to persuade Japan to attack its 'old enemy' the Russians. (Japan had won the Russo-Japanese War in 1904-05 when both countries clashed over claims to territory in the decaying Chinese empire.) However, the Japanese did not welcome the thought of their troops fighting in the frozen wastes of Siberia just to please Hitler since they had made plans of their own that would inevitably lead to war with the United States and Britain.

When Hitler realised he could not count on the Japanese for military support, relations between the two countries cooled to such an extent that the German embassy in Tokyo was not kept informed about Japan's last-minute negotiations with the United States as they balanced precariously on the brink of war. When the Japanese attacked Pearl Harbour the Germans only came to know about it after listening to a broadcast from Radio Tokyo.

With the 'freezing' of Japanese assets in the US and the cutting off of US oil exports to Japan, the United States and Japan began to intensify preparations for war. In the process the possibility of a Japanese surprise attack on Pearl Harbour was considered a possibility.

In July 1941 President Roosevelt signed an order nationalising the armed forces in the Philippines and

THE JAPANESE INVASION OF SOUTHEAST ASIA

BURMA

THAILAND
(Siam)

Bangkok

FRENCH
INDO-CHINA
(Occupied 1940)

Saigon
(Ho Chi Minh City)

HAINAN
(Occupied 1940)

PHILIPPINE
ISLANDS

Manila

Patani & Singora (Siam)
Kota Bahru (Malaya)
Invaded 8 Dec. 1941

MALAYA

SINGAPORE

SUMATRA

DUTCH EAST INDIES

Batavia
(Jakarta)

JAVA

BORNEO

CELEBES

NEW GUINEA

appointing General Douglas MacArthur the Commanding General, US Armed Forces, Far East.

The world was stunned by the news that the US Pacific Fleet had been crippled at Pearl Harbour in a well-planned sneak attack by Japanese carrier-based planes. At about the same time of the Pearl Harbour attack, Japanese troops began invading the beaches at Kota Bahru in north-east Malaya. Other Japanese troops who had landed at Singora and Patani in south-east Siam (Thailand) had cut westwards across the country to invade the state of Kedah in north-western Malaya. They moved swiftly southwards, capturing important towns, railway junctions and airfields, easily pushing aside disorganised British resistance.

On 31 January 1941 Johore, the southern-most Malayan state, was occupied by the Japanese army and the dispirited and battered remnants of British defenders were withdrawn across the Johore Causeway to Singapore for a final 'last stand'.

A week of intensified artillery and air bombardment of Singapore followed during which the supply of water from Johore to Singapore was cut off, a vital factor that hastened Singapore's surrender.

Japanese troops of the 25th Army under the command Lt.-Gen. Tomoyuki Yamashita crossed the Straits of Johore on 8 February 1942 and invaded Singapore.

Seven days later, Lt.-Gen. Arthur E. Percival, Commander of British Forces, surrendered Singapore unconditionally at the Ford Motor Factory in Bukit Timah.

Lt. Gen Arthur E. Percival, GOC, Malaya Command.

A shocked and angry Winston Churchill, the British Prime Minister, had promised a 'full inquiry' for Singapore's surrender that he described as 'the worst disaster and largest capitulation in British history'.

Such an inquiry was never held.

The actual number of Chinese executed in The Singapore Chinese Massacre will never be known nor will the number of Chinese who died *after* the 'screening and registration' that began on 18 February 1942 and 'officially' ended two weeks later, on 4 March.

The persecution of innocent Chinese continued relentlessly until the surrender of Japan in 1945.

Chapter 1

Grim Reminders Of War

'There was no room for the Japanese Army to counter-argue the charge of the inhumane murders in which countless Chinese were executed indiscriminately on the beaches, in rubber plantations and in the jungles without investigations or trials. There was no justification for the massacres even if some Chinese had fought us as volunteers and collaborated with anti-Japanese elements.'

Lt.-Col. Iwaichi Fujiwara, war historian, commenting on The Singapore Chinese Massacre.

On 15 February each year, two memorial ceremonies are held in Singapore, at the Kranji War Memorial and the Civilian Memorial beside Raffles City to commemorate the surrender of Singapore to the Japanese that ended more than a century of British colonial rule. It was Britain's most humiliating military defeat.

At the Kranji War Memorial are the graves of some 24,000 military servicemen .

The Civilian Memorial in Beach Road is in memory of the unknown number of civilians of all races who were victims of the Japanese Occupation from 1942 to 1945; a very large number having died under terrible circumstances, the most notorious being The Singapore Chinese Massacre.

KRANJI WAR CEMETERY 1939-1945

The imposing entrance to the Kranji War Cemetery in Singapore, which contains the remains of British and Allied troops who died during the Japanese invasion of Malaya and Singapore in 1941-42

For many years there had been unsuccessful demands by the Chinese communities in Singapore and Malaya (following the surrender of Japan in 1945) for official apologies (yet to be made) and compensation from the Japanese government for the numerous atrocities by the Japanese army in Singapore, Malaya, Borneo and Sarawak.

The Japanese government had maintained that since Singapore and Malaya were under British rule at the time of the Japanese invasion there were 'no legal grounds' for making such claims.

Eighteen years later, in September 1963, the Japanese agreed that each of the thirteen states that comprised Malaysia (which at that time included Singapore) would receive 10 million (Malaysian *ringgit*) as payment of a 'blood debt'.

However, demands for more compensation continued and the Japanese agreed to make a 'gift' of 25 million (Malaysian *ringgit*) and 25 million (Singapore dollars) to the Malaysian and Singapore governments respectively.

Among the many thousands who were executed in the Singapore massacre were Chinese refugees from Malaya who had fled to Singapore believing in the British claim that the island was an 'impregnable fortress'.

As mentioned earlier in the *Introduction*, the remains of the victims of the massacre that were found in shallow graves by War Crimes investigators in Singapore after the surrender of Japan, fell far short of the figure (5,000) admitted by the Japanese War Office in Tokyo.

Chinese community leaders had pointed out that in addition to the massacred victims, groups of Chinese suspected of being members of the Anti-Enemy Back Up Society that had the support of the Malayan Communist Party (MCP) were executed after the massacre had 'officially' ended on 4 March 1942 and continued up to the time of Japan's surrender in 1945.

Following the surrender of Singapore, the Japanese Military Administration on the instructions from the *Kempeitai*, demanded a 'donation' of $50 million from the Chinese communities in Malaya and Singapore as a 'safeguard against further mass arrests and executions'.

Chinese leaders such as Dr Lim Boon Keng and other prominent Chinese personalities were detained and ordered by the *Kempeitai* to form an association and a fund-raising committee. When $10 million (Singapore's share) was paid to the Japanese Military Administration, it was widely publicised as 'a voluntary gesture by the Chinese to demonstrate their co-operation and friendship towards Japan' (see chapter 8: *The $50 Million 'Donation'* page 74).

Dr Lim was born in Singapore in 1869 and died in 1957. He was educated at Raffles Institution and became the first Chinese in Singapore to receive in 1887, a 'Queen's Scholarship' to study medicine at Edinburgh University. He was also an educationist and a founder of the Singapore Chinese Girls' School. He strongly believed in a Chinese education and taught himself to read and write the language. He founded the Straits Chinese British Association. When World War II broke out in Europe in 1939, Dr Lim campaigned for funds for the British war effort. He was awarded the Order of the British Empire (OBE).

The Japanese were also eager to arrest tin and rubber tycoon, educationist and philanthropist Tan Kah Kee and to execute him. Tan in his capacity as chairman of the Singapore China Relief Fund committee Southseas (Southeast Asia) China Relief Fund Union and president of the region's United Overseas Chinese Relief Fund had collected millions of dollars in aid for General Chiang Kai-shek, the Nationalist leader. Tan and his family had escaped from Singapore to Sumatra with British help shortly before the surrender of Singapore. From Sumatra he went to Java where he remained until the surrender of Japan. Tan who was born in Fujian province in China, died in his homeland in 1961 at the age of 76.

Other prominent members of the Chinese, Malay, Indian and Eurasian communities were selected by the *Kempeitai* to become 'leaders'. They had no choice of refusal. Officers of the Japanese Military Administration were powerless to overrule orders by the *Kempeitai*.

The people who were selected as 'leaders' of their respective communities agreed to accept the appointments because of fear of reprisals against them, their families and their communities since the *Kempeitai* had established a notorious reputation before, during and after the Singapore massacre.

Often Chinese leaders as well as those from the Malay, Indian and Eurasian communities were arrested by the *Kempeitai*, beaten up and released with warnings that they had to 'demonstrate their gratitude to the Japanese army for liberating them from being slaves of the British colonial imperialists'.

Community leaders were forced to read speeches prepared by the Japanese Military Administration's Propaganda Department that would condemn the 'evil British colonialists' and praise the 'noble and invincible' Japanese.

On occasions when such speeches were read, officers from the *Kempeitai* posing as civilians were among the audiences. If the speakers appeared 'unconvincing', they were obliged to spend a few days at a *Kempeitai* detention centre to witness people being tortured for 'failing to cooperate'.

A prominent Singapore lawyer remarked after the surrender of Japan in 1945:

'The British colonial authorities had the audacity to accuse Singapore community leaders of "collaborating with the enemy" by pledging their loyalty and the loyalty of their communities to the Japanese. A number of British civilians might also have been accused of "collaboration" for working in various capacities for the Japanese after the surrender of Singapore. Some were not even interned during the whole period of the Japanese Occupation. Immediately after the surrender of Japan, the British authorities sent these people out of Singapore to avoid a scandal. Why weren't British government officers and those in the private sector in Malaya and Singapore charged with disloyalty and desertion after they had jumped on to evacuation ships reserved for women and children? What happened in Penang in December 1941 was a disgrace. Non-European women and children were prevented from evacuating and British men, women and children escaped on trains leaving for Singapore. We thought such a thing would not happen in Singapore, but it did, repeatedly. After the war, the British chose to describe these desertions as 'escapes'. The local people had remained loyal to the last in Singapore. The British had no idea of the terror we experienced under the Japanese. Look what happened during the Chinese massacre and the atrocities against local people who had refused to welcome the Japanese as "liberators". We lived in constant fear of torture and death by the *Kempeitai*. The British did not seem to realise that Singapore's population which was largely made up of British subjects, had in fact become prisoners-of-war and were exposed to arrest and unspeakable torture by the *Kempeitai* who prowled the streets by day and night with an insatiable thirst for human blood.

The British appeared to be more concerned with the rehabilitation of their economic interests, restoring trade to Singapore and reviving tin and rubber production in Malaya. This was because at the end of World War II, Britain was almost bankrupt and needed funding from its colonial possessions. I don't believe the British learnt any lessons from their humiliating defeat by the Japanese. On their return to Singapore they wished to be welcomed as our "liberators". While we were happy to see them back and that the terror of the Japanese Occupation had ended, I think they were expecting a little too much.'

Chapter 2

Uncertainty And Suspicion

There was a feeling of uncertainty and suspicion among sections of the population of Singapore at the time of The Singapore Chinese Massacre Trial that the British authorities were anxious to 'play down' the massacre since it occurred almost immediately after the humiliating surrender of Singapore.

Suspicions especially among the Chinese community increased when claims for compensation because of the massacre were tactfully dismissed along with requests that an inquiry be set up to discover the actual number of Chinese who were executed.

A Chinese newspaper columnist had commented: 'If the Japanese had massacred some 300,000 Chinese civilians over a period of six weeks in Nanking in 1937, weren't they capable of executing 50,000 Chinese over a period of two weeks in Singapore? The Japanese would admit they had reason to hate Chinese more than they hated the British. They regarded every Chinese a danger to Japanese life and property, as had happened in China after the Japanese takeover of Manchuria in 1931. Massacres became a part of life in China. The Japanese decided to execute many thousands of Chinese in Singapore for the purpose of causing fear and alarm among the Chinese community, which they succeeded in doing.'

It was also felt the British wished to put their defeat by the Japanese behind them and restore their 'lost face' especially among the Chinese on whom they largely depended to restore Singapore's pre-war position as a trading and financial centre. Similarly, the British also needed the Chinese in Malaya to help rehabilitate the once booming tin and rubber industries that were in shambles because of the Japanese Occupation and also to revive their various chambers of commerce.

In order to achieve this it was important that painful memories of massacres and tortures suffered by the Chinese at the hands of the Japanese were soon forgotten by Chinese communities in both territories since they would only remind them of the fact that they were badly let down and deceived by the British prior to and during the Japanese invasion.

In an indirect way to 'heal' wounded Chinese feelings the British authorities in Singapore and Malaya supported Chinese claims for 'blood debts' and compensation from the Japanese government for losses suffered during the war.

Chapter 3

A New Terror

The surrender of Singapore in February 1942 had ended the horrors of war between the two adversaries. But the civilian population was to face a terror far worse than they had yet experienced. It was the constant fear of arrest, unspeakable torture and possible death that would haunt them each day for three and a half years, until the surrender of Japan.

This fearsome 'spectre' was the *Kempeitai*, the Japanese secret/military police and an 'army' of local informers comprised mostly of secret society gangsters who were released from prison and recruited by the *Kempeitai* (see End Notes: *Kempeitai Tortures* page 110) It was the job of these informers to pick out people whom they considered, for whatever reason, to be 'anti-Japanese', knowing they could be sending each person to a terrible death.

As victorious Japanese troops entered the city on that fateful day, units of the *Kempeitai* had already begun an island-wide, house-to-house search for 'anti-Japanese elements' among the Chinese population.

The *Kempeitai* were aware that among the Chinese community in Singapore were those who supported the communist-led Malayan Peoples Anti-Japanese Army

(MPAJA) that was in the jungles of Malaya fighting a guerrilla war against Japanese troops in conjunction with Force 136, comprised of British army officers and officers attached to the Malayan police force. Force 136 also included Malayan and Singapore Chinese espionage agents who were trained in guerrilla warfare in India and secretly sent back to Malaya by submarine or had parachuted into the jungles.

One such secret agent was Lim Bo Seng who was taken to India by the British before the surrender of Singapore. He returned to Malaya by submarine in November 1943 and was arrested by the *Kempeitai* in March 1944. He died from torture in a Malayan prison in June the same year. (His memorial is at the waterfront Esplanade in Singapore).

Immediately after the surrender of Singapore, Gen. Yamashita, commander of the victorious 25th Army, divided Singapore into four sectors. The elite Konoye Imperial Guard Division commanded by Lt.-Gen. Takuma Nishimura was put in charge of the eastern half of Singapore. The city and its surrounding area were in charge of Maj.-Gen. Saburo Kawamura that included the notorious No.2 Field *Kempeitai* that would soon figure prominently in The Singapore Chinese Massacre, two battalions of infantry and five independent companies for guard duties. The north and western sectors of Singapore were under the command of Lt.-Gen Takeo Matsui and Lt.-Gen. Renya Mutaguchi respectively.

With these forces in place, Gen. Yamashita quickly issued an order to his four area commanders in which he stated that all male Chinese between the age of eighteen and fifty-five were to assemble at various places throughout the island on 18 February for the purpose of being 'screened and registered'.

The man who had devised the plan for the 'screening and registration' and who would carry out Gen.Yamashita's order was Lt.-Col. Masanobu Tsuji, who was Yamashita's Chief Planning Officer. (Mention was made of Tsuji in the *Introduction* of this book and the bizarre methods that he and the *Kempeitai* had used in selecting thousands of innocent people for execution.)

While preparations were being made to carry out Col. Tsuji's 'master plan' for revenge against the Chinese population, Japanese troops known as *Hojo Kempei* (those temporarily attached to the 'regular' *Kempeitai*) were conducting their own 'screening' in other parts of Singapore; at checkpoints, bridges and road intersections in their relentless search for 'anti-Japanese Chinese elements'.

The 'suspects' were young Chinese males.They were placed in lorries and taken to the Tanjong Pagar Railway Station where they were locked up in wooden cages used for transporting cattle, before being sent to slave labour camps in the jungles of Siam (Thailand) and Burma (Myanmar).A few who had survived torture,starvation and disease returned to Singapore after the war to tell of their harrowing experiences in these camps that were also inhabited by nationals from other Japanese-occupied countries.

It was at these 'sentry checkpoints' that the people of Singapore were introduced to a side of Japanese character they had not seen among the Japanese community in Singapore before the Pacific War. It was a complete opposite of the polite Japanese shop assistants at the 'Tokyo ten-cent stores' in the Middle Road and Waterloo Street areas and the bowing waiters and kimono-clad waitresses at *sukiyaki* restaurants.Their visions of these pleasant and cultured people were instantly shattered when they were confronted by scowling Japanese sentries who took great delight in face-slapping, shin-kicking or ramming the butts of their rifles into the faces of those who did not bow 'respectfully' to them as 'representatives of the Emperor' who had 'liberated' the people of Singapore from 'the evil British imperialists'.

Most Japanese troops had not met Malays, Indians and Europeans before. Up to the time of the invasion of Malaya, the only foreigners they had come in contact with were 'the Chinese enemy' in China and whom they now faced again in large numbers in territories in Southeast Asia. This was because young Japanese army recruits were sent directly from Japan to join army units in China.

Broadcasts from 'Radio Syonan' (*Syonan* meaning 'light of the south' in Japanese, and the new name given to Singapore) and articles in the *Syonan Times* newspaper that were obviously directed at the Chinese population, warned that 'anti-Japanese elements' would be 'severely punished'. (When the Japanese used the term 'severely punished' it meant 'severe torture and death'.)

The *Kempeitai* were everywhere, in military uniform at checkpoints or dressed as Chinese 'coolies', coffee-shop waiters or hawkers. Many were fluent in Chinese dialects and in their enthusiasm to arrest 'anti-Japanese Chinese' wore monks' robes and mingled with worshippers at Taoist and Buddhist temples from where 'suspected anti-Japanese elements' were arrested, beaten up and taken away in waiting lorries to face an unknown fate.

Mothers shaved the heads of their teenage daughters and dressed them in boys' clothes, fearing they would be forced to become 'sex slaves' in brothels run by the Japanese army for their troops. It had been a practice of the Japanese army to 'recruit' young women for this purpose in territories under their control, from   Korea that became a Japanese colony in 1910, to occupied countries in Southeast Asia. (The horrible experiences of these women have been published in several books and made into films.)

People in Singapore began to distrust old friends or even relatives, some of whom had been forced to work for the *Kempeitai* as informers. Those who showed a lack of 'enthusiasm' in performing their duties were detained and severely beaten. Families of those who had 'disappeared' and believed to have been arrested by the *Kempeitai* were afraid to make inquiries at police stations for fear of being arrested and tortured.

The YMCA building in Orchard Road; the Cockpit Hotel in Oxley Rise (off Orchard Road); the Central Police Station in South Bridge Road and a former private residence in Smith Street in Chinatown, were used as *Kempeitai* command centres. Branches were also established in all other districts.

Cells for prisoners and torture chambers were quickly constructed at each branch.

Chapter 4

Gen. Yamashita's Dilemma

And The POW Problem

Gen. Yamashita and his divisional commanders' knowledge of administering occupied territory had been restricted to towns and villages in China. They now faced the bewildering task of solving urgent problems to maintain essential services in Singapore, a cosmopolitan city and one of the world's most important air and sea hubs.

Gen. Yamashita.

Singapore's population was 500,000 at the outbreak of war, of which about 400,000 were Chinese. The remainder was made up of Malays, Indians, Eurasians and a small number of Europeans. This figure was doubled by an influx of refugees, mostly Chinese from Malaya, eager to reach the safety of Singapore that the British had described as 'an impregnable fortress'.

The threat of cholera and typhoid epidemics caused by decomposing bodies of British and Japanese soldiers in Singapore's reservoirs was a growing danger not only to the civilian population but to Japanese troops garrisoned on the island as well as those who were about to take part in the invasions of Sumatra and Java. Also, Gen. Yamashita was concerned about the threat of sabotage and guerrilla warfare by Chinese volunteers of Dalforce who were believed to be still at large.

Another of his worries was the fate of some 130,000 British, Australian and Indian prisoners of war (POWs) a problem that had never confronted the Japanese army in China since captured or surrendered Chinese troops were executed or sent to slave labour camps.

The Japanese believed that soldiers should die fighting 'like heroes'. Only cowards surrendered and should be killed.

When Emperor Hirohito had commanded his armed forces to surrender after the Americans had atom-bombed Hiroshima and Nagasaki in August 1945, his 'divine' order was largely obeyed. However, there were some who had refused to lay down their arms and committed *hara-kiri* or *seppuku* (ritual suicide according to the ideals of *bushido*, the code of the *samurai*.)

There was no excuse for a Japanese soldier to be taken prisoner. He was expected to find some way to kill himself so that his spirit would dwell at Yasukuni (meaning 'peace and tranqulity') Shrine in Tokyo, the resting place of all heroes. It was built by the Emperor Meji in 1869 to honour some 3,600 soldiers who had died fighting the warlords to restore Imperial rule.

> **Note:** At the International Military Tribunal (Far East) set up in Tokyo after the surrender of Japan in 1945, three classes of war crimes and criminals were defined:
> **Class A:** Top Japanese officials who had conspired to wage war and committed the most heinous crimes such

as murder, ill-treatment of prisoners-of-war, rape, pillage and the cruel treatment of civilians. **Class B:** Top officers who had ordered atrocities to be committed by their troops and had themselves participated in these atrocities. **Class C:** Prison guards and lower ranking military personnel accused of abusing prisoners-of-war. In 1978 the Japanese government had inducted into Yasukuni Shrine seven Class A war criminals who were hanged after being found guilty of crimes by the Military Tribunal in 1948. They were: **Hideki Tojo:** Japan's wartime prime minister. He assumed full responsibility for the actions of his government and the armed forces. **Kenji Doihara:** Troop commander in Singapore from 1944–45 and was in control of civilian internee camps. **Koki Hirota:** He was foreign   minister during the Nanking Massacre in 1937 and was prime minister 1936-37. He helped plan the invasion of Southeast Asia and the war in China. **Seshiro Itagaki:** Commander of Japanese forces in Singapore in 1945 and controller of food and medical supplies to prisoner-of-war camps. **Heitaro Kimura:** Army commander who helped plan the China and Pacific wars, He allowed prisoners-of-war to be tortured and was in charge of the Siam-Burma 'Death' Railway in which thousands of prisoners and civilian 'slave-labour' died. **Iwane Matsui:** Commander of troops who were responsible for the Nanking Massacre. **Akira Muto:** Commander of troops that took part in the Nanking Massacre and a massacre of civilians in Manila.

It was not surprising therefore, why the Japanese had shown such contempt for Allied troops whom they looked upon as 'inferiors and cowards' for not committing suicide instead of surrendering. This attitude may account for the brutal treatment of surrendered or captured Allied servicemen in Malaya and Singapore and in other theatres of the Pacific War. It may also explain their brutality towards the civilian populations in territories that came under their control.

As much as the Army High Command in Tokyo may have wished to have solved the 'Allied prisoner-of-war problem' in a similar manner as they had done with captured or surrendered troops in China, they had realised the world was watching them after their sensational victories in Southeast Asia and the Pacific. They had apparently thought it would be wise to avoid any indiscriminate action on their part, although they had already committed atrocities against wounded British, Australian and Indian troops during the fighting in Malaya, as was revealed at War Crimes trials.

The Japanese, however, had other ways of getting rid of the 'prisoners-of-war problem', by enforcing 'death marches' in which prisoners starved, had no water and medical attention, as happened in the Philippines and Borneo and by using prisoners as 'slave labour'; the Burma-Siam 'Death' Railway being an example.

Of a total of 46,000 prisoners-of-war who worked on the 'Death Railway' that included members of the Singapore Volunteer Corps (SVC), some 16,000 died of disease, torture or starvation. Their graves are at Kachanaburi and Thonburi in northern Thailand, beside the River Kwai where they had slaved and died while building the notorious bridge that was the subject of a film, *Bridge On The River Kwai*.

Gen. Yamashita had given top priority to finding a quick way to eliminate 'anti-Japanese elements' among the

Chinese population in Singapore. While he was busy seeing to the security of Japanese troops who would be staying on in Singapore to maintain law and order, he was also making final preparations for the invasion of Java and Sumatra. He was obliged to leave details for the 'screening and registration' of Chinese civilians to his Chief Planning and Operations Officer, Lt.-Col. Masanobu Tsuji.

> **Note:** In 1929 in Geneva, Japan was among the signatories to the provisions set out in the International Convention Relative to the Treatment of Prisoners of War. The Japanese, however, had not formally ratified it when they attacked Pearl Harbour on 7 December (Hawaiian Time) 1941. Japanese accused of war crimes at International Military Tribunals and War Crimes Courts after the war, claimed in their defence that since Japan had not ratified the Geneva Convention, they did not have to comply with its terms and conditions for the proper treatment of prisoners of war and therefore could not be charged with the atrocities they were accused of having committed. This claim was rejected. It was noted that Japan had signed The Hague Convention of 1907. One of the provisions was that the lives and property of inhabitants of occupied territories had to be respected.

Chapter 5

War Criminals Are Charged

After the surrender of Japan in 1945, British War Crimes investigators in Singapore began the task of gathering evidence to prosecute Japanese guilty of atrocities against civilians, particularly those involved in The Chinese Massacre.

On 10 March 1947 The Chinese Massacre Trial began before a British Military Court at the Victoria Memorial Hall, presided over by five judges.

The court was informed that executions from 18 February to 4 March were carried out mainly at beaches at Punggol, Changi, Teluk Mata Ikan and Tanah Merah Besar, Siglap and Tanjong Katong (near the old Chinese Swimming Club). Also at the Tanjong Pagar wharves (along the west coast) and the island of Belakang Mati (now Sentosa).

Accused of the massacre were seven high-ranking Japanese officers. They were:

- Maj.-Gen. Saburo Kawamura, commander of the Singapore garrison.
- Lt.-Gen. Takuma Nishimura, commander of the Imperial Guards Division and Lt.-Col. Masayuki Oishi, head of the *Kempeitai*.
- Other *Kempeitai* officers charged were: Lt.-Col. Yoshitaka Yokota, Maj. Tomotatsu Jyo, Maj. Satorou Onishi and Capt. Haruji Hisamatsu.

They were all found guilty.

Japanese defence lawyers told the court that the 'screening and registration' of Chinese civilians after the surrender of Singapore should be regarded as a 'military operation' because as army officers, the accused were expected to automatically carry out orders passed down to them by their superiors. They pointed out that a Japanese soldier would prefer to die rather than disobey an order. The officers whom they defended had obeyed orders given by their superior officers; the orders originating from Gen. Yamashita.

Gen. Nishimura in his defence said he had been 'too busy' preparing his troops for the imminent invasion of Sumatra and could not take part in the 'screening and registration'. He said the whole operation, including the executions, were the responsibility of Lt.-Col. Tsuji.

Gen. Kawamura in his defence said he had been informed on 23 February, five days after the operation began, that about 5,000 Chinese had been executed. He had personally told Gen. Yamashita about the number who had been killed. He said Gen. Yamashita had remarked that he 'did not think that all the anti-Japanese elements had been killed' and insisted the massacre should continue.

Gen. Kawamura and Col. Oishi were hanged at Changi Prison.

Gen. Nishimura, Col. Yokota, Maj. Jyo, Maj. Onishi and Capt. Hisamatsu were sentenced to life imprisonment, the first five years of their sentences to be served in Singapore and the remainder in Japan.

There were immediate protests from the Chinese community who felt the court had 'appeared to accept too easily' the Japanese claim that only 5,000 were executed.

A Singapore Chinese Appeals Committee was formed.

They claimed at least 50,000 were executed and demanded that all seven accused who had been found guilty, be hanged in public.

The committee was subsequently informed that re-trials and changes to original sentences imposed by War Crimes (military) Courts were not permitted and appeals could not be lodged in civil courts.

> **Note:** While Gen. Nishimura was serving a life sentence in 1950, he was arrested by Australian war crimes investigators and charged before an Australian military court for ordering the execution of Australian and Indian prisoners-of-war during the fighting in the state of Johore in south Malaya in January 1941. He was found guilty and hanged.

The number of Chinese executed was disputed from the start at the Massacre Trial.

Lt.-Col. Ichiji Sugita, Chief of Intelligence attached to General Yamashita's 25th Army headquarters, said 5,000 Chinese were killed in February 1942.

However, a sworn statement by a Domei News Agency correspondent, Takafumi Hishikari, was presented at the trial in which he stated that Col. Sugita had told him that 50,000 Chinese who were suspected of being communists and anti-Japanese, were going to be killed. He said Col. Sugita informed him later that 'it had not been possible to kill 50,000 as had been intended — but, 25,000 had been massacred.' Hishikari also said in his statement that Major Tadahiko Hayashi, an Intelligence Staff Officer, had told him that 25,000 Chinese had been executed.

Chapter 6

The Massacre

Of the thousands of Chinese massacred, only few who were to be executed by Japanese firing squads suffered bullet wounds and escaped by pretending to be dead. They told of their experiences at the Singapore Chinese Massacre Trial. It was believed that other executions took place from 18 February and 4 March 1942 in addition to those mentioned at the Massacre Trial. These were not brought before the Court because survivors or witnesses had died during the Japanese Occupation. Also, because senior Japanese army and *Kempeitai* officers had refused to disclose information of the massacres.

Two days before the 'official' date (18 February 1942) for the Chinese 'registration and screening' operation to begin, a massacre of Chinese had already taken place.

It happened on **16 February**.

A *Kempeitai* unit under the command of a Capt. Haruji Hisamatsu backed by about a hundred soldiers had occupied the Tanjong Pagar Police Station, on the day following the surrender of Singapore. (Capt. Hisamatsu was found guilty at The Chinese Massacre Trial and sentenced to life imprisonment).

The local police at the station had been informed that all Chinese suspected of being anti-Japanese were to be killed. Chinese residents were assembled at three points: Tiong Bahru, the junction of Cantonment and Neil roads and at the Singapore Harbour Board 'coolie' lines.

Each day, large groups of Chinese were taken away in lorries with their hands tied behind their backs. They were beheaded at the Tanjong Pagar wharves. Also, motor launches packed with Chinese and guarded by armed *Kempeitai* soldiers were seen to stop some distance from Pulau Belakang Mati (Sentosa Island). The occupants were pushed overboard and shot. Hundreds of bodies, many headless, were washed ashore on the island and also at the site of the Royal Singapore Yacht Club at Tanjong Pagar.

More than 700 Chinese who had been under detention by the *Kempeitai* at various locations in the area were brought to the Tanjong Pagar Police Station between **17 and 24 February** with their hands tied behind their backs. They were taken away in lorries in batches of about thirty and executed. Some were picked out because they had tattoo marks on their bodies. Some of the tattoos were of religious significance but the Japanese preferred to believe they were the symbols of secret societies. The victims were not interrogated before being sent to their deaths.

Details of this atrocity were given in evidence at The Singapore Chinese Massacre Trial by two inspectors of the Singapore Police Force. Arthur John and Thomas Issac were stationed at the Tanjong Pagar Police Station when the massacres took place. Inspector John said Capt. Hisamatsu had told him that Chinese in the Tanjong Pagar area were to be rounded up and concentrated at certain points. John said he saw several headless bodies floating near the Tanjong Pagar wharves. He also said that the Japanese were offering rewards for information leading to the arrest of prominent members of the Chinese community who were in hiding.

The War Crimes Court heard evidence from the few who had survived the massacres and from eyewitnesses. The evidence revealed:

Three mass executions took place on **23 February**.

The first account was given by Lee Siew Kow who witnessed a massacre at the beach near the Chinese Swimming Club at Amber Road in Tanjong Katong, on the east coast.

Lee, who lived near the beach, said he saw three lorries with Chinese civilians pass his house. The lorries stopped and those on the lorries were ordered to get off by armed Japanese guards. There were about fifty male Chinese and all had their hands tied behind their backs. The Japanese guards divided them into groups of three and marched them to the beach where they were made to kneel facing the sea. All were shot by rifle fire. Those who were still alive were stabbed to death with bayonets or *samurai* swords.

Another massacre on **23 February** took place at the 7th milestone, East Coast Road.

Khoo Ah Ling, who was one of those selected to be killed, managed to escape. He told the War Crimes Court that he was ordered to go to the Teluk Kurau English School on **20 February** where he joined about 3,000 other Chinese between the ages of sixteen and fifty who had assembled at the school's playing field. Those who had admitted to the Japanese that they owned property valued at $50,000 and more, were asked to stand aside. Khoo did not know what became of them. Other groups were made up of schoolteachers, high school students, members of the

Hainanese community and Chinese who had lived in Malaya for less than five years.

Khoo said all those who had assembled were taken to the school building and locked inside classrooms. In each classroom there were about two hundred people.

The following day, without any questions being asked, the Japanese tied them in pairs with rope and put them into lorries. They were taken to the 7th milestone Siglap Road and roped together (about fifty to a group) and marched to a hill some distance from the main road.

As they were climbing the hill Khoo managed to loosen the rope around his hands and ran towards the nearby jungle as the guards fired shots, but none hit him. He ran to a friend's house in nearby Changi where he found shelter. He said none of his friends who were roped together with him were seen alive again. He presumed that they and all the others were killed.

Also on **23 February**, the victims of another massacre at East Coast Road were buried in shallow graves. A woman named Ang Ah Mui who had been ordered by the Japanese to dig trenches the day before the killings, said groups of Chinese were roped together and made to stand in front of the trenches. As they were shot, they fell backwards into the trenches. When she returned to the scene of the massacre some days later she saw the personal belongings of the victims scattered on the ground. The shallow trenches had been filled with earth and had attracted packs of hungry, stray dogs.

On **18 and 20 February** Chinese civilians living in the Jalan Besar area were ordered to assemble at the Victoria School playing field. The *Kempeitai* quickly picked out about 800 people who were massacred at Mata Ikan, a village on the east coast. Another execution was at Tanah Merah later, also on the east coast.

A witness, Wong Peng Yin, was among hundreds who had been ordered to assemble at Victoria School. He and others were taken in lorries by Japanese guards to a beach near Changi Prison. He said:

'When we got off the lorries the Japanese guards tied us in fives and we were then marched down to the beach. When we got there I noticed some dead bodies lying there. They were all Chinese. As soon as I got into the water my rope loosened and then we were marched about two hundred yards from the shore. The Japanese guards who had remained on the beach, opened fire with machine-guns and rifles. I had managed to struggle out of my ropes and swam away in the direction of Mata Ikan (village) where I waded ashore and spent the night in a squatter's house. As far as I know, only one other in my group escaped and he was wounded.'

Another who survived a massacre was Chua Choon Guan, one of about 350 victims who were taken to a beach at Tanah Merah to be killed. On arrival they were roped together in batches of eleven and made to stand in the sea close to the shore. The guards opened fire with machine-guns. Everybody, except himself was killed. He said:

'They were all machine-gunned and I presume they died because I never saw them again. I was in the fifth row to be machine-gunned. The bullets hit me but I was not killed. I fell and the others who were shot dead fell on top of me. I was almost unconscious and then I felt a hard blow on my head that made me completely unconscious. When I regained consciousness it was dark. I had come to because the tide had come in and the waves lapped against my face. I was still bound but I found a sharp rock near the beach and was able to cut the rope by rubbing it against the rock. I then crawled way and escaped.'

On **19 February**, Captain Kosaki Goshi who was a

Kempeitai officer, rounded up several thousand Chinese and assembled them at the junction of Ord Road and River Valley Road for 'screening and registration'. First to be taken away in lorries for execution were about 400. They were shot at beaches in the Changi area.

Capt. Goshi was sentenced to death by a War Crimes Court in Kuala Lumpur for committing atrocities in Malaya. He was hanged at Changi Prison.

On **28 February**, Lt.-Gen. Takuma Nishimura, commander of the Imperial Guards Division, was sentenced to life imprisonment at the Chinese Massacre Trial. He was later found guilty of atrocities by an Australian court and hanged in 1951.

He had rounded up a large number of Chinese in the Upper Serangoon Road area of Singapore at the time of the 'screening and registration' operation. More than 1,000 Chinese were taken in lorries to Oehlers' Lodge at the 11th mile Punggol Road. They were made to kneel in groups of about 300 in the large garden beside the sea where they were machine-gunned. When the beach and garden became littered with corpses, groups of other victims were taken to a nearby rubber plantation and shot. Two of the victims made a break for freedom and got away. A large number of bodies were thrown into the sea. The Japanese found it to be a more convenient way of disposal than burying bodies in shallow graves. One of the survivors said:

'We were taken in a lorry to a place about nine miles away where we were stripped and inspected for tattoo marks. From there we were taken by lorry to the 11th mile Punggol Road where there were eleven lorries full of Chinese guarded by about a hundred Japanese soldiers. After being made to kneel down for about twenty minutes in the garden of a bungalow near the seashore, eighteen of us were marched by the Japanese guards over the road into a field near a rubber plantation. The leader of the guards wrote in the sand that he was our "saviour". We thought he was giving us an opportunity to escape and we quickly ran up a small hill into the plantation. Shots were fired at us but all except two of us got safely away.'

Another massacre on **28 February** involving 90 former Chinese members of the Singapore Volunteer Corps (SVC) was carried out at the beach at Bedok on the east coast. Chan Cheng Yean was shot in the knee and pretended to be dead. He later crawled out from under the corpses of his comrades and escaped after the Japanese machine-gunners had left.

On the afternoon of **1 March** while he was at a village in Teluk Mata Ikan off Changi Road, Tan Hai Sar saw several covered lorries arrive. The lorries were filled with Chinese who had their hands tied behind their backs. They were taken to a nearby beach and shot. Other lorries arrived with more victims. The killings went on day and night. Tan said he saw some cars with Japanese soldiers arrive. After inspecting some air-raid trenches near his house, the soldiers left. A few hours later he saw lorries filled with about four to five hundred Chinese. They were roped together in small groups and made to kneel in front of the trenches. Tan, who was hiding behind a tree said the victims were killed by machine-gun fire. Their bodies fell into the empty trenches.

Tan said, 'I heard the cries of those who had not been killed. I visited the scene of the massacre some days later. The stench of rotting bodies was unbearable because they had fallen into shallow graves. Some farmers and I reburied the bodies in deeper graves.'

By **2 March**, Gen. Yamashita's orders had been fully

carried out by Lt.-Col. Tsuji, assisted by the *Kempeitai* and troops under the four divisional commanders.

PUNGGOL BEACH MASSACRE

The inscription on the plaque (above) erected by The National Heritage Board, Singapore, reads:

"On 23 February 1942, some 300-400 Chinese civilians were killed along the Punggol foreshore by 'hojo kempei' (auxiliary military police) firing squad. They were among tens of thousands who lost their lives during the Japanese 'Sook Ching' operation to purge suspected anti-Japanese civilians among Singapore's Chinese population between 18 February and 4 March, 1942. The victims who perished along the foreshore were among 1,000 Chinese males rounded up following a house-to-house search of the Chinese community living along Upper Serangoon Road, by Japanese soldiers."

CHANGI BEACH IN PRE-WAR DAYS
One of the sites where the massacres took place

CHANGI BEACH MASSACRE

The inscription on the plaque (above) erected by
The National Heritage Board, Singapore, reads:

"66 Chinese male civilians were killed by Japanese 'hojo kempe'
(auxiliary military police) firing at the water's edge on this stretch of
Changi Beach on 20 February, 1942. They were among tens of
thousands who lost their lives during the Japanese 'Sook Ching'
operation to purge suspected anti-Japanese civilians within Singapore's
Chinese population between 18 February and 4 March, 1942.
Tanah Merah Besar Beach, a few hundred metres south (now part
of the Changi Airport runway) was one of the most heavily- used
killing grounds where well over a thousand Chinese men and youths
lost their lives."

Chapter 7

'Terrified People'

Mamoru Shinozaki was Press Attache at the Japanese consulate in Singapore before the Pacific War began. In 1940 he had been sentenced to three and a half years in prison after a trial at the Supreme Court on charges of 'collecting information which might be useful to a foreign power'.

Evidence at his trial had shown that a year before Japan invaded Hong Kong and countries in Southeast Asia, Shinozaki had taken a party of high-ranking Japanese army officers who were posing as tourists, to view 'sights' in Singapore and Malaya. Among the 'scenic attractions' were areas close to British fortifications, such as the Naval Base in Singapore, in which the visitors had shown an unusually keen interest.

Shinozaki had denied he was a spy and claimed he was unaware of the 'true identity' of the 'tourists'. A soft-spoken and affable man, he had made a large number of friends in Singapore, including Chinese and Europeans, before his imprisonment.

He was released from Changi Prison by the victorious Japanese 25th Army and given a senior position with the Japanese Foreign Affairs Department in Singapore. In this capacity he offered his protection to thousands of Singapore residents, mostly Chinese, by issuing them with 'passes' bearing his signature.

He had also obtained the release of several prominent local residents who had been detained by the *Kempeitai* among them the well-known Chinese leader Dr Lim Boon Keng, with whom he later set up the Overseas Chinese Association. The association was primarily concerned with the protection of Chinese in Singapore and to which Shinozaki became an adviser.

After the war Shinozaki wrote a book *My Syonan, My Story* ('Syonan' was the name the Japanese gave to Singapore. It meant 'light of the south').

He had devoted a chapter entitled 'The Chinese Massacre' in which he stated that shortly after the British had surrendered Singapore, an order was signed by General Yamashita that all male Chinese had to be 'screened and registered'. According to Shinozaki, the 'screening and registration' operation was the 'brainchild' of Col. Tsuji (of whom much has been written elsewhere in this book).

Shinozaki in his evidence at The Singapore Chinese Massacre Trial asserted that Col. Tsuji had also advised Gen. Yamashita on how the massacres should be carried out.

Describing the reaction of the Chinese community to Gen. Yamashita's order that they were to be 'screened', Shinozaki wrote: 'There was fear and trembling in every Chinese home. What did this order mean?'

The *Kempeitai* had earlier begun searching Chinese homes throughout Singapore and had been arresting large numbers of Chinese, including women, even before Gen. Yamashita's order was made known.

Shinozaki revealed that at the 'screening and registration' centres there was no food, drinking water or toilets and people waited in the sun and rain for days in the hope of being given

'SOOK CHING' REGISTRATION CENTRE
IN CHINATOWN

The inscription on the monument reads:

"The site was one of the temporary registration centres of the Japanese Military Police, the 'Kempeitai', for screening 'anti-Japanese' Chinese.

On 18 February 1942, three days after the surrender of Singapore, the 'Kempeitai' launched a month-long purge of 'anti-Japanese elements' in an operation named 'Sook Ching'. All Chinese men between 18 and 50 years old, and in some cases women and children, were ordered to report to these temporary registration centres for interrogation and identification by the 'Kempeitai'.

Those who passed the arbitrary screening were released with 'Examined' stamped on theis faces, arms or clothes. Others not so fortunate were taken to outlying parts of Singapore and executed for alleged anti-Japanese activities. Tens of thousands were estimated to have lost their lives.

For those who were spared, the 'Sook Ching' screening remains one of their worst memories of the Japanese Occupation a rubber stamp on their shirts or arms to show they had been 'registered' and had been 'approved'.

'Thousands were massacred during this notorious operation,' said Shinozaki. 'Some of the victims were told to write their names. Some wrote in English, some in Chinese. Those who knew English were at once classified as being "pro-British and dangerous". Those with tattoo marks were classified as being "members of secret societies". Those who were unable to write their names in Chinese and who could not explain why they had tattoo marks, were also slaughtered.'

He went on to say that the *Kempeitai* had discovered lists with the names of anti-Japanese organizations in Singapore and also the names of important members of the China Relief Fund and the Chinese volunteer regiment, 'Dalforce'.

'With this discovery came a new terror,' said Shinozaki. 'The *Kempeitai* began a wave of arrests! The Chinese community lived in fear of a knock on the door! Arrest! Detention! Death! Only high-ranking Japanese officers would know how many were massacred.'

Chapter 8

The $50 Million 'Donation'

Towards the end of The Singapore Chinese Massacre in March 1942, the *Kempeitai* discovered through their informers, lists with names of Chinese who had belonged to anti-Japanese organizations such as the China Relief Fund, 'Dalforce' and secret societies whose members were used in the enforcement of boycotts of Japanese goods.

Several prominent Chinese businessmen and community leaders were arrested and there were fears they would be executed. Among those detained was Dr Lim Boon Keng.

The documents seized by the *Kempeitai* included a file in which there was a clipping from a newspaper showing a photograph of Dr Lim with a Nationalist Chinese military delegation from Chungking which had visited Singapore. Also in the file was a letter from the Nationalist Chinese leader, Gen. Chiang Kai-shek, thanking Dr Lim for the hospitality he had shown the visitors.

The *Kempeitai* officer in charge of Dr Lim's case was Lt.-Col. Yoshitaka Yokota, who was sentenced to life imprisonment at the Chinese Massacre Trial.

Mamoru Shinozaki (see *Terrified People,* page 70) in his evidence at the Chinese Massacre Trial said Col. Yokota had informed him about Dr Lim's arrest. He had asked Col. Yokota not to treat Dr Lim harshly since he was seventy-two years old and was his friend.

Dr Lim and Shinozaki had met previously to discuss ways of easing pressure by the *Kempeitai* on the Chinese population. At their meeting, Shinozaki had suggested to Dr Lim that a Chinese association be formed which would make efforts to convince the Japanese Military Administration in Singapore and the *Kempeitai* in particular, that the Chinese should not be treated as enemies as so far had been the case. Dr Lim felt that such an association might offer some sort of protection to the Chinese community from being persecuted by the *Kempeitai*.

On Col. Yokota's advice and with approval from the Military Administration, the Overseas Chinese Association was formed. This resulted in the release of a number of prominent Chinese who were under detention by the *Kempeitai*.

Secretly, the Japanese planned to make the fullest use of the Chinese Association and Shinozaki's efforts to change the attitude of anti-Chinese factions in the Military Administration, failed. These 'die-hard' Japanese officers' hatred for the Chinese had developed while they were serving with the Kwantung Army in Manchuria.

They had decided there should be no preferential treatment shown to the 'Chinese enemies' in Singapore. They would be treated in the same way as 'anti-Japanese' elements in China. It had to be clearly understood that the Chinese were enemies of Japan, no matter where they happened to be.

However, the Administration had hinted that the Chinese 'should demonstrate their desire for co-operation and friendship with the Japanese' by making a 'voluntary donation' of $50 million through the Association.

Chinese community leaders and businessmen were summoned to a meeting including those who had been arrested and who were still showing the effects of the months of torture by the *Kempeitai* while they were under detention. To avoid being re-arrested and tortured again, they were prepared to do whatever they were told. The presence of these men at the meeting also reminded those Chinese who may have not wished to support the idea of a 'voluntary donation' to the Japanese that it would be prudent on their part to show their willingness to contribute towards it, however much they were against doing so.

The 'donation' would be made by the Chinese residents of Malaya, who would be expected to contribute $40 million, the other $10 million coming from the Singapore Chinese community.

The meeting was held under the chairmanship of an official named Takahashi who was an adviser to the Military Administration. It had also been decided that Chinese property owners in Singapore and Malaya would each have to contribute eight per cent of the value of their properties.

Many of those who were approached for 'donations' were widows whose husbands were executed during the 'screening and registration' operation in February 1942. The widows were told 'to make donations in the names of their deceased husbands'. Whatever their hidden feelings were, these unfortunate women knew better than to refuse.

Takahashi had made it clear to all those present at the meeting that the *Kempeitai* was determined to execute every Chinese in Singapore and Malaya and that it would be better to 'pay or be killed'.

The Singapore Chinese community succeeded in raising their share of $10 million. However, the Malayan Chinese were only able to raise $18 million of the $40 million expected from them. The deficit of $22 million was 'borrowed' from the Yokohama Specie Bank by the Military Administration on behalf of the Malayan Chinese.

The *Kempeitai*, who had been monitoring the Overseas Chinese Association's 'fund-raising' meeting very closely, suspected some of the widows of the men who had been executed in the Singapore Chinese Massacre had not told the truth about their financial status and had buried jewellery and cash in British currency, as many wealthy families had done before the Japanese occupied Singapore.

Several of these women were arrested by the *Kempeitai* and tortured. Some were not seen again.

End Notes

Tsuji: 'Master-mind' Of The Massacre

Japanese army commanders were unanimous in their evidence at The Singapore Chinese Massacre Trial in March 1947 that Lt.-Col. Masanobu Tsuji was the 'brains' behind the operation and had personally supervised each stage of the executions.

His colleagues had described him as 'brilliant, daring and sinister'. Indeed, these were important characteristics to

Tsuji, the politician, after the surrender of Japan.

possess if he was to excel among the lot of aspiring, young cadet officers at the Tokyo Military Academy in 1934 from where he graduated with top honours and the rank of captain.

He was an ardent supporter of the Control Faction of a political group known as the Imperial Way that advocated army rule and total loyalty to the Emperor. In was around this time that he discovered a coup was being hatched by some of his cadet friends whom he betrayed and exposed to a senior officer attached to Imperial Headquarters. Tsuji had done it in such a way that the counter-coup would come to the attention of Hideki Tojo (then a major-general) and leader of the Control Faction.

Tojo rewarded Tsuji for his loyalty when he became wartime prime minister of Japan by granting him certain privileges that officers of more senior rank were not allowed.

Senior army officers in their evidence at The Singapore Chinese Massacre Trial said Tsuji had over-stepped his authority and committed acts of insubordination that Gen. Yamashita was obliged to overlook because of Tsuji's influence with Imperial Headquarters in Tokyo, headed by Tojo. Tsuji had issued orders during the massacre with Yamashita's knowledge but without his approval. This had convinced senior officers that Tsuji was Tojo's spy.

While Japan's invasion plans of Southeast Asia were being stepped up during the early part of 1941, Gen. Yamashita was commander of the Kwantung Defence Army in Manchuria. His sudden appointment as commander of the 25th Army that would invade Malaya, Singapore and the Dutch East Indies called for the appointment of an officer with the ability to plan and co-ordinate the army's campaigns.

Malaya and Singapore were two valuable prizes to be won. Malaya produced about 40 per cent of the world's rubber and about 60 per cent of the world's tin while the capture of Singapore with its great naval base would eliminate Britain's military power in the Far East.

Tsuji was Gen. Tojo's automatic choice to fill the important position as Chief Planning and Operations Officer of the 25th Army. Tsuji was already in Formosa (Taiwan) where he was in charge of an army research station and busily engaged in logistics planning and co-ordinating espionage information in preparation for the forthcoming invasion of Malaya and Singapore.

Late in 1941 Tsuji was in Saigon (Ho Chi Minh City) that was occupied by Japanese troops. As the war in Europe raged, German forces had swept through France. The puppet (Vichy) French government appointed by Hitler had allowed Japanese troops to enter the former French colonies of Vietnam, Cambodia and Laos and to build air bases. (Japan was a member of the 'Axis Powers' that comprised Germany and Italy.)

> **Note:** It was from air bases in Vietnam that Japanese planes carried out a surprise raid on Singapore in the early hours of 8 December 1941. Two days later, on 10 December, Vietnam-based torpedo-bombers sank the battleship *Prince of Wales* and the battle-cruiser *Repulse*, off Mersing on the south-eastern coast of Johore. Both ships were the main strength of the British Far Eastern Fleet.

The enterprising Tsuji was promoted to the rank of lieutenant-colonel after he had won the admiration of his superiors for daring spying missions in which he flew over the coastal towns of Singora and Patani in south-eastern Siam (Thailand) and the strategic British air bases at Kota Bahru in the north-eastern Malayan state of Kelantan and Alor Star in the north-western state of Kedah.

> **Note:** The beaches at Singora, Patani and Kota Bahru were invaded by Japanese   troops early on 8 December 1941 at the start of the campaign in Malaya. Three British air bases in Kelantan were captured within a few hours. Other Japanese army divisions cutting across southern Siam invaded Kedah in north-west Malaya, occupying British air bases at Alor Star, Butterworth and Penang that had been evacuated before the arrival of Japanese troops.

Tsuji had not only planned the Japanese military campaign in Malaya aided by information provided by a network of spies, but also the type of punishment 'anti-Japanese elements' principally among the Chinese population, would receive.

Even before Japan went to war and as Japanese army commanders were finalising their plans for invasion, Tsuji was so confident of Japanese victories in Malaya and Singapore that he had asked for a list of names of 'anti-Japanese elements' in the two territories that had been compiled by Japanese secret agents.

The list was 'up-dated' by the time the Japanese had occupied Ipoh, the capital of the north-western Malayan state of Perak, early in January 1941.

With this information in hand he began planning the *Sook Ching* ('purification by purge') operation to eliminate 'anti-Japanese elements' among the Chinese community in Singapore. His fears about such elements would have increased greatly after guerrillas of the (mainly Chinese) Malayan Peoples Anti-Japanese Army (MPAJA) and Force 136, a British guerrilla unit, had ambushed and set ablaze a train in the state of Perak filled with hundreds of troops of the Japanese 18th Division.

Tsuji may have been reminded of the tenacious resistance put up by Chinese guerrillas in northern China after the Japanese takeover of Manchuria in 1931.

However, he was yet to witness another example of heroic Chinese resistance when Dalforce went into action against Japanese troops that had invaded Singapore on 8 February 1942.

Tsuji was a man of extraordinary ingenuity and courage. Some of his superstitious colleagues in the 25th Army believed he possessed supernatural powers that he used on his superior officers so that they would agree with his views on important issues.

Tsuji was in Burma at the time of the surrender of Japanese troops to British forces in August 1946 and slipped away to Siam where he wandered about disguised as a Buddhist monk. After a spell in China, he returned to Japan and became a politician. He was elected to the Japanese Diet (parliament).

His few friends had described him as 'brilliant, ingenious and mysterious', generously omitting that he was also 'cunning, ruthless and barbaric'.

Tojo's Plea Of Innocence

General Hideki Tojo, the Japanese prime minister was hanged in Tokyo in 1948 after being found guilty of war crimes by an International Military Tribunal. He was described as 'the most prominent and most blameworthy of all the major Japanese war criminals'.

During his interrogation in March 1946 he said that since the end of the war he had read about the 'inhumane acts committed by the Japanese army and navy that were certainly not the intention of those in authority, namely the General Staff, the War or Navy Departments, including himself'.

He went on to say:'We did not even suspect that such things had happened. The Emperor, especially, because of his benevolence, would have had a contrary feeling. Such acts are not permissible in Japan; the character of the Japanese people is such that they believe that neither Heaven nor Earth would permit such things. It will be too bad if people in the world believe that these inhumane acts are the result of Japanese character.'

The War Crimes Tribunal in Tokyo had heard evidence from a large number of witnesses who gave detailed accounts of tortures and atrocities by the Japanese and on a scale so vast that only one conclusion was possible: that the atrocities were either secretly ordered or wilfully permitted with the knowledge and consent of the Japanese government and by the leaders of the armed forces.

Japanese Prime Minister Tojo

The Tribunal had ruled that Tojo was responsible for Japan's criminal attacks on her neighbours and for the ill-treatment of prisoners-of-war and civilian internees. It said the barbarous treatment of prisoners and internees and civilians was well known to Tojo. He took no steps to punish offenders and to prevent such crimes in China and in Japanese-occupied territories.

Bringing War Criminals To Trial

Identifying, locating and arresting thousands of suspected Japanese war criminals became the responsibility of the British and American authorities. The Americans set up a war crimes organization in Tokyo and the British one in Singapore. While the concern of these organizations was mainly to deal with war crimes against their own nationals, all evidence against suspects was shared with investigators in other countries that had been under Japanese occupation.

British investigations were conducted by General Headquarters, Allied Land Forces, Southeast Asia. These covered Singapore, Malaya, Siam (Thailand), French Indo-China (Vietnam, Cambodia and Laos), Burma (Myanmar), Hong Kong, Tientsin, Shanghai, British North Borneo (Sabah), the Netherlands East Indies (Indonesia) and the Andaman and Nicobar Islands.

The organization came under the control of the Judge Advocate General's Branch that was directly responsible to the Military Deputy of the Judge Advocate General in London.

By February 1948, a total of 931 Japanese war criminals were tried.

The American investigating organization in Tokyo acted under the United States Joint Chiefs of Staff who ordered the investigations, arrest and detention of all suspected Japanese war criminals. Provision was also made for the handing over of all war criminals wanted by other countries. The directive also empowered Gen. Douglas MacArthur, the Supreme Commander of Allied Powers, to establish special international courts and rules to be followed. The military commanders of any nation taking part in the occupation of Japan were also authorized to set up military courts for the trials of war criminals.

The American investigations covered: Burma (Myanmar), Siam (Thailand), French Indo-China (Vietnam, Cambodia and Laos), Malaya, Singapore, Sumatra, Java, Borneo (Sabah) and the Celebes.

They Fought To The Last Man

After the surrender of Singapore, the victorious Gen. Yamashita placed sections of the island under the control of his divisional commanders. British, Australian and Indian troops who had retreated from Malaya to Singapore had laid down their arms and the British civilian population of some 4,000 was awaiting internment at Changi Prison. But, what worried the Japanese High Command were the unknown number of enemies; the saboteurs and spies and other 'anti-Japanese elements' among the Chinese population.

The Japanese had intended keeping only a small number of troops to maintain law and order in Singapore and move their main force to attack Sumatra and Java. Before doing so, they had wished to make sure the troops they had left behind for garrison duties would not be attacked by a tenacious volunteer force known as Dalforce.

Dalforce or 'Dalco' was made up of a number of Chinese who had been active in anti-Japanese operations in areas around Kuala Lumpur until the city fell in January 1941. The guerrillas not only carried out sabotage, but also fought side-by-side with British army units. Most of them were poorly armed, using shotguns, hunting rifles and even axes and *parangs*. They fought to the last man, realising if they were captured they would be tortured and executed.

Dalforce included many volunteers who had been released from Changi Prison. They had been convicted in

British courts for being communist activists. Others were loyal to Gen. Chiang Kai-shek, the Nationalist Chinese leader. Upon their release they underwent training by Lt.-Col. John Dalley, a former police officer in Malaya after whom the force was named.

They had fought courageously in the Kranji area northwest of Singapore, after the main force of Japanese troops had crossed the Straits of Johore on 8 February 1942. In the creeks and mudflats between the Australian positions and Kranji, Dalforce volunteers awaited for the first wave of enemy invasion troops. Although outnumbered, they fought fierce hand-to-hand battles to the last man in the face of Japanese air and tank attacks.

The bravery of these men might have caused some embarrassment to the British colonial administration in Singapore headed by Sir Shenton Thomas, the governor, who had been deeply suspicious of any attempt to organise guerrilla units made up of Chinese, Malays and Indians that could operate against the Japanese in towns as well as in the jungles in each state in Malaya. These units would be led by British police officers, rubber planters and tin miners who spoke Malay and were also familiar with the terrain. Detailed plans submitted as early as August 1941 were at first rejected and approved shortly before the Japanese invasion, when the British suddenly realised it would be to their advantage to get the 'locals', especially the Chinese, on their side against the Japanese.

'The Battle For Singapore':
The Point Of No Retreat

There was no panic; no 'stunned silence' at the news on the evening of 31 January 1942 that British, Australian and Indian troops had been withdrawn from Johore Bahru, capital of Malaya's southern-most state (across the Causeway from Singapore) and that the 'Battle For Singapore' had begun.

Following almost two months of 'running battles' also known as 'strategic withdrawals' in war communiqués from Malaya Command Headquarters, the people of Singapore and Malaya had become used to hearing unpleasant news 'toned down' by pleasant-sounding synonyms such as 'withdrawal' instead of 'retreat' and 'evacuated' instead of 'abandoned'. Example: Penang was 'evacuated' (not 'abandoned') to the Japanese (without a fight!) as were Kuala Lumpur, the Federal capital, Seremban the capital of Negri Sembilan and Malacca.

'Would someone tell us what's really going on?' had probably been the most-asked question in the various languages spoken in cosmopolitan Singapore and Kuala Lumpur since the Japanese invasion at Kota Bahru in Kelantan on 8 December 1941.

At times one had to assume where battles were being fought or to which area a 'strategic withdrawal to prepared positions' by the defenders was made. But, one thing seemed quite certain: The Japanese were coming closer to Singapore, faster than they themselves had probably imagined.

They ruled the sea — with the sinking of the battleship *Prince of Wales* and battle-cruiser *Repluse* two days after their invasion began.

They ruled the land — towns and airbases in the north were 'successfully evacuated' before the arrival of the Japanese whose rapid advance was halted at Kampar and the Slim River in Perak where they suffered heavy losses before continuing to 'breeze' through pockets of disorganised British resistance.

Half of Malaya was in Japanese hands.

Other Japanese army units had moved down the east coast of Malaya from Kota Bahru in Kelantan (where the invasion began) and had, almost unopposed, come as far as Endau in Johore.

The Japanese ruled the air, too. Whatever obsolete British aircraft that had escaped destruction on the ground in Japanese bombing raids had been 'successfully transferred' to Java, leaving the ground forces exposed to aerial machine-gunning, dive-bombing and attempting to repulse infantry attacks supported by tanks and artillery fire.

This was the grim scenario from the start of the Japanese invasion.

Nobody could, with any justification, have blamed the tired and sleep-starved British, Australian and Indian defenders who had arrived in Johore Bahru and were 'withdrawn' to Singapore on 31 January for having lost their will to put up a 'gallant last-stand' to save Britain from its worst military defeat in history — a fact that British Prime Minister Winston Churchill was well aware of.

In the 'early days' of the war, the Japanese air force had

raided Singapore with squadrons made up of a modest twenty-seven bombers. But, after occupying abandoned ('evacuated') airbases in north and central Malaya, they began raiding Singapore with up to 156 bombers whenever they felt like it, the pilots flying well above the range of anti-aircraft guns. Dive-bombers and fighter-bombers operating from bases in Malacca and northern Johore joined in the round-the-clock attacks on Singapore.

What about damage caused by the bombings and the loss of civilian life? — questions that everyone was asking.

A typical communiqué from Command Headquarters in Singapore usually issued 24 hours after a bombing raid would read as follows: 'Enemy bombers visited the north and south-western areas of Singapore Island yesterday, causing damage and casualties.' There might also have been a vague communiqué about 'enemy action in Malaya' and about 'our troops occupying prepared positions after inflicting heavy casualties on the enemy.'

Newspaper reports about the war were consequently vague and 'padded' with trivia and unimportant 'background' material since no journalists and photographers other than those permitted by Malaya Command Headquarters were allowed anywhere near battle areas.

Would someone tell us what's really going on?

That question was now being asked in outbursts of rage following the first bit of stimulating news that broke the monotony of the terse official announcements.

It was about a well-laid ambush in northern Johore on 14 January (only seventeen days before Gen. Percival withdrew his forces from Johore Bahru to Singapore) in which Australian troops had killed some 700 Japanese of the Mukaide Detachment. It was the biggest loss suffered by the Japanese in any single action and it was felt that the long-awaited turning point in a one-sided war had finally arrived.

There was wild speculation that with the sensational (and confirmed) Australian victory, 'the Japs would from now on be on the run with the Aussies hot on their heels!'

Then came the news of the withdrawal of British forces to Singapore.

'What the hell's going on! We kill seven hundred Japs! Then, when it looks as though we're winning for the first time, we withdraw!' said an irate, grey-headed English *tuan* while sheltering under a dining table at the 'Europeans only' Singapore Swimming Club during a heavy Japanese air raid. 'Somebody should tell those buffoons at Command Headquarters that the idea is to keep the Japs away from Singapore and not invite the bastards in!'

The Australian ambush

Maj.-Gen. Gordon Bennett, Commander of the Australian Imperial Forces (AIF) was in command of 'Westforce,' a new line of defence from east to west in northern Johore. On 10 January he had inspected the Gemencheh River and the wooden bridge that spanned it, located just above the railway junction town of Gemas. Bennett had chosen the spot for a major ambush against advancing Japanese troops on their way south towards Singapore. Ambush positions were taken up by men belonging to the 2/30th Battalion of the Australian 27th Brigade.

At about 4 pm on 14 January an advance force of some 300 Japanese troops on bicycles crossed the bridge and entered the 'killing zone' further down the road that the Austalians had prepared. They were joined by 500 others, also on bicycles. It was then that the Australians blew up the bridge. In a fast and furious battle 700 Japanese lay dead and several of their tanks destroyed. Australian losses were eight dead and 80 wounded. The Australians continued with a follow-up operation, mopping up the remnants of the Japanese force.

A week later on 21 January, to the west of the Gemencheh River, Australian and Indian troops successfully halted the advance of a strong Japanese force supported by artillery, tanks and fighter planes. In bitter hand-to-hand fighting for possession of a strategic bridge at Parit Sulong losses on both sides were heavy, the Japanese also losing several tanks. The heroic action by the Australians and Indians allowed time for the major strength of 'Westforce' to regroup and strengthen their defences. Lt.-Col. Charles G.W. Anderson of the Australian 2/19th Battalion who was in command, was awarded the Victoria Cross for his bravery and leadership.

These actions had proved that the Japanese advance could be effectively stopped and heavy losses inflicted on them under proper direction. But, as much as Gen. Percival might have wished for a counter-offensive led by Gen. Bennett, he would have realised he had the heavy responsibility of reserving whatever troops he could for the fast-approaching 'Battle For Singapore' in an attempt to save British 'face' and an 'impregnable fortress' from humiliating surrender.

The realisation that Japanese troops were about to take up positions on Singapore's 'doorstep' in Johore Bahru had prompted British Prime Minister Winston Churchill to send an urgent message on 20 January to General Sir Archibald Wavell, Supreme Commander, Allied Command, Far East, saying: 'I want to make it absolutely clear that I expect every inch of ground to be defended, every scrap of material for defences to be blown to pieces to prevent capture by the enemy, and no question of surrender to be entertained until after protracted fighting among the ruins of Singapore City.'

Fighting words from 10,000 miles away in London! But what Churchill didn't know was that Wavell had discovered very little had been done to strengthen Singapore's northern defences and it was too late now to do anything about it. To add to the confusion, newly-recruited British troops were arriving in Singapore — and nobody seemed to know what to do with them! A few crates containing Hurricane fighter aircraft had also arrived — too late to be of any use since there was nobody to assemble them — or pilots to fly them! The morale of troops was low and the whole defensive pattern as Wavell saw it, was in pretty poor shape.

Singapore's civilian population had doubled to a million with the influx of refugees from Malaya and food supplies were running short. Another of Percival's big concerns was the mounting number of civilian casualties from increased Japanese air bombardment. He was also aware that the supply of water to Singapore from Johore could be cut off at any time once Japanese troops captured the Gunong Pulai waterworks.

The beginning of the end

31 January 1942.

The scene: The waterfront at Johore Bahru.

British troops had departed after blowing a hole in the Causeway in the hope of delaying Japanese tanks and army vehicles from crossing over to Singapore. Japanese army engineers quickly repaired the damage.

As night fell, Japanese troops looked across the Straits of Johore for a first glimpse of the Singapore coast and at the huge, black 'oil cloud' from burning diesel storage tanks at the giant Seletar Naval Base that had been set alight by the British before abandoning it some weeks before. The reason for this was to deprive the Japanese of precious oil supplies.

Japanese troops were in jubilant mood. Soon they would be celebrating a memorable victory in 'fortress' Singapore.

From the tower of the Sultan of Johore's grand palace overlooking the Straits of Johore, Gen. Yamashita focused his binoculars on the shores at Kranji in northern Singapore. But he was in no hurry to begin his invasion — for good reason. He realised his supplies of food and artillery ammunition were very low and his invasion force of some 30,000 troops would soon be facing 130,000 British troops whom he expected to put up tenacious resistance to save their 'impregnable fortress.'

Yamashita had to take a chance for a quick victory. A prolonged battle would be a disaster — and an irrecoverable 'loss of face' for him. He spent the next few days in conference with his divisional commanders.

On 6 February, he issued final orders for the invasion.

It would begin on the evening of 7 February with a cunning 'dummy' attack by a unit of the Imperial Guards Division directed at Pulau Ubin, an island off the eastern tip of Singapore. It would be carried out in order to make British defenders pay less attention to the beaches along the northern coast where the actual invasion would begin.

Yamashita would wait until early the following day (8 February) to direct his main attacking forces (the 5th and 18th Divisions) across the Straits of Johore towards the Kranji areas in northern and north-western Singapore. Once the invasion was in full swing, the main force of the Imperial Guards Division would cross the Straits and begin landings in the Woodlands area west of the Causeway.

Yamashita reckoned that the Japanese flag would be flying over Singapore within four days.

As planned, he launched his invasion on 8 February.

Australian machine-gunners defending the north-western ad western sectors of Singapore where the Japanese 5th and 18th Divisions concentrated their attack, mowed down wave after wave of the invaders, who despite suffering heavy losses, were finally able to come ashore.

Later, Yamashita set up his headquarters in a rubber plantation near Tengah airbase where he was surprised to discover several undamaged aircraft, uneaten food on dining room tables and clothes scattered in the barracks, indicating that a hurried evacuation had taken place.

Japanese troops made some advances while a fierce artillery battle was raging. Japanese gunners kept up an incessant barrage although they were running dangerously short of ammunition. But, it was part of Yamashita's bluff to make Gen. Percival believe that his artillery units had a plentiful supply of shells.

On 10 February, Yamashita was expecting to come up against stiff resistance at Bukit Timah Hill but to his surprise the British defenders seemed disorganised and were retreating in confusion.

After paying a final visit to the battle areas before leaving for his headquarters in Java, Gen. Wavell sent an urgent message to Churchill: 'Battle For Singapore not going well. Morale of some troops not good. I have given the most categorical orders that there is to be no thought of surrender and that all troops are to continue fighting to the end.'

11 February: Japanese 5th Division troops continued their advance eastwards along Jurong Road and southwards. They took control of Bukit Timah Village.

There were bitter hand-to-hand fighting and bayonet charges in which men of the Australian 22nd Brigade suffered heavy casualties. Japanese Imperial Guards who had earlier broken through the Australian 27th Brigade defending Woodlands, pushed aside what was left of the Kranji-Jurong line of defenders and were headed towards the Peirce and MacRitchie reservoirs. On the Chua Chu Kang Road, Japanese 5th Division troops advanced towards Bukit Panjang Village.

12 February: Japanese 5th Division troops supported by tanks advanced down the Bukit Timah Road while British and Indian troops clashed with the advancing Imperial Guards Division who had already captured MacRitchie and Peirce reservoirs.

In western Singapore in the Pasir Panjang area, men of the 1st Battalion Malay Regiment and the 44th Indian Brigade stopped advancing troops of the Japanese 18th Divison in their attempts to capture the huge British supply depot at Alexandra Barracks. The Japanese suffered heavy casualties as they come up against Malay Regiment machine-gunners. Heavy fighting continued and the Japanese were reinforced with tanks.

On 13 February, Percival told Wavell that he would not be able to hold out for more than two more days since Japanese bombers had damaged the reservoirs and the water supply system — and there was no hope of restoring the supply. He implied that continued fighting would only produce needless suffering. Wavell replied: 'You must continue to inflict maximum losses on the enemy for as long as possible by house-to-house fighting if necessary.'

Fighting was still going on during the morning of 15 February.

Yamashita was with Gen. Renya Mutaguchi,

commander of the 18th Division and as they stood on high ground on Upper Bukit Timah Road, Yamashita noticed through his binoculars, that several British artillery positions had been silenced by fierce dive-bombing attacks the previous day. Mutaguchi's troops had meanwhile advanced along the west coast of Singapore and were moving in towards the city.

Yamashita gave orders that his artillery units would keep on firing until the very last round and his troops would continue their advance at whatever the cost.

This could have been Yamashita's 'last stand' before he completely exhausted his ammunition and food supplies. He was unaware that his bluff had worked and that Percival was ready to surrender.

Yamashita must have breathed a long sigh of relief when a forward unit of the 18th Division noticed a white flag had been hoisted on a tree on Caldecott Hill near the Radio Malaya broadcasting studios. Later, a car displaying a white flag was seen moving towards the Japanese lines.

Lt.-Col. Ichiji Sugita, Yamashita's Chief Intelligence Officer, met the occupants of the car — all senior British officers — who had come to discuss surrender terms.

Surrender

Yamashita was suspicious of the British officers and demanded to see Gen. Percival. At 5.15 pm that evening Percival arrived with two of his staff officers and an interpreter (Major Wild).

They were taken to a room at the Ford Motor Factory in Upper Bukit Timah Road that had become Yamashita's headquarters.

After Yamashita's interpreter had made the formal introductions, the two opposing commanders shook hands and sat down at a table facing each other.

According to a Japanese version of the meeting, the dialogue was as follows:

Yamashita: Answer me briefly. Do you wish to surrender unconditionally?

Percival:Yes...we do.

Yamashita: Have you any Japanese prisoners of war?

Percival: No.They have all been sent to India.

Yamashita:Very well.Will you please sign this document of surrender?

Percival began to read it. He stopped and asked Yamashita:

Percival:Would you wait until tomorrow morning?

Yamashita (angrily): If you don't sign now we shall go on fighting. All I want to know is: Do you surrender unconditionally or do you not?

*Percival went pale and began talking to the interpreter in a low voice.Yamashita pointed a finger at Percival and shouted:

Yamashita:Yes or no?

Percival glanced towards the interpreter before replying.

Percival:Yes.

Yamashita: Very well. We shall cease hostilities at 10 pm Japanese Time.

Percival then asked Yamashita not to allow his troops into Singapore city until the following morning (16 February).This was to give Percival time to inform all his army units and the civilian population of the surrender.Yamashita agreed.

Percival:What about the lives of the civilians and the British and Australian troops? Will you guarantee them?

Yamashita: Yes. You may be easy about that. I can guarantee them, absolutely.

The surrender document was signed at 6.10 pm.

*Yamashita later denied he had shouted at Percival. He said he became angry with his interpreter for making mistakes. He said he had wished to treat Percival courteously.

★ ★ ★

After the humiliating surrender of Singapore to 'filthy, stinking Jap coolies in army uniform!' (as one English *mem* had described Japanese soldiers) Churchill had promised a full-scale inquiry into the causes of the historic capitulation.

Apparently he had good reason to change his mind, because such an inquiry was never held.

BRITISH TROOPS SURRENDERING TO THE JAPANESE

NORTH AND WESTERN SECTOR   NORTH AND EASTERN SECTOR

JOHORE

NIGHT OF 7 FEB.
Imperial Guards Div.
make 'dummy' attack.

PULAU UBIN

CHANGI

2nd Bn. MALAY REGT

3rd INDIAN CORPS

BEDOK

KALLANG
AIRPORT

PUNGGOL

18th DIVISION

SELETAR
AIR BASE

Seletar Reservoir

Peirce Reservoir

MacRitchie Reservoir

FORTRESS
FORCES
(SVC)

Straits of Johore

SEMBAWANG

NAVAL
BASE

11th DIVISION

SEMBAWANG
AIR BASE

CAUSEWAY

27th BRIGADE

Imperial Guards

5th DIVISION

KRANJI

MANDAI

BUKIT PANJANG

BUKIT TIMAH

18th Division

1st Bn. MALAY REGT

PASIR PANJANG

BELAKANG MATI

JOHORE BAHRU

IMPERIAL GUARDS

5th DIVISION

TENGAH
AIR BASE

18th Division

CHUA CHU KANG

22nd BRIGADE

JURONG

INDIAN 44th BRIGADE

LIM CHU KANG

JOHORE

5th DIVISION

18th DIVISION

2/19th Battalion

Straits of Johore

Japanese Forces

British Forces

Australian Forces

Japanese Advance

The Day Singapore Surrendered

S ome people became hysterical and committed suicide while others burst into tears or drank themselves senseless when told on the evening of 15 February 1942 that the 'unthinkable' had happened: *The British had surrendered Singapore!*

Yet, others laughed at the news. It was a cruel joke they said or 'just another stupid rumour', like the one that said 'a hundred British fighter planes were due in Singapore at any moment from Australia'. The rumour came at a time when Japanese troops were advancing along Bukit Timah Road and Japanese snipers were seen perched on trees in the Botanic Gardens.

Some hours before Singapore surrendered, another rumour said that 'thousands of Nationalist Chinese troops supported by tanks had landed at Mersing on the east coast of Johore. The Japanese were now trapped between British troops in Singapore and Chinese troops racing towards Johore Bahru.'

Desperate people were prepared to believe anything that might have given them even the slightest glimmer of hope for Singapore's survival. Eyes that had seen so much bloodshed, death and suffering searched the skies, waiting for the 'miracle' appearance of the British planes from Australia that would save Singapore and for news about the 'counter attack by Nationalist Chinese troops'.

Nothing more was heard.

And then... the 'unthinkable' happened.

Quite suddenly, 'the little men from the Land of the Rising Sun' as they were known by some English *tuans* and *mems*, were the new masters of Singapore!

On the morning before the surrender, the only aircraft in the skies were Japanese as they went about their 'routine' machine-gunning and dive-bombing of a city that was dying of shame and its wounds.

British troops had been without air support from the beginning of the Japanese invasion of Malaya on 8 December 1941. Planes at air bases in Malaya and Singapore mostly used for reconnaissance were withdrawn to Java, not that the few and mostly obsolete World War I aircraft would have been any match for the 'secret weapon' of the Japanese air force, the sensational 'Zero' fighter.

British, Australian and Indian troops were withdrawn from Malaya across the Johore Causeway to Singapore on 31 January 1941. General Yamashita, commander of the victorious 25th Army, rested his troops in Johore Bahru and from the tower of the sultan's grand palace he could see the heavy layer of black smoke from the burning fuel tanks at the giant Naval Base. They were set ablaze by the British before evacuating the base weeks before Japanese troops reached Johore Bahru. It was done to deprive the Japanese of precious oil supplies.

General Yamashita was expecting a tough battle that he secretly realised he could lose, since his troops were outnumbered by at least four to one, and because he was running desperately short of ammunition and other supplies. It was imperative that victory was won in the shortest possibletime.

Yamashita's fears of a prolonged battle for Singapore

might have been increased after Winston Churchill, the British prime minister, in a special broadcast from London declared that the surrender of 'fortress Singapore' was 'unthinkable' and that 'it would be defended to the last surviving man and woman'.

British Prime Minister Winston Churchill,

Nothing like that happened.

The Japanese invasion of Singapore began on 8 February. Seven days later, the one-sided 'Battle for Singapore' ended when a humiliated General Percival surrendered Singapore, unconditionally.

Hours before Singapore surrendered, exuberant Japanese 'Zero' fighter pilots sensing British resistance was at its end flew so low, their faces could easily be seen. Some even waved to startled people taking shelter in open air-raid trenches. The vibrations from their planes' engines rattled and dislodged tiles on the roofs of shop-houses in Chinatown as the planes roared crazily towards the Tanjong Pagar wharves where the captains of the last evacuation ships were hoping to escape. A short distance away, three coastal ships with mostly women and children aboard were on fire. To add to the horror of the scene, the survivors struggling in the sea were being machine-gunned by 'Zero' pilots. Installations on the southern islands of Pulau Belakang Mati (Sentosa Island) and Pulau Berani were on fire as were the oil storage tanks on Pulau Bukom from which rose huge, spiralling yellow and black clouds of smoke. They linked up with the massive and almost stationary heavy, black cloud formed by burning oil from storage tanks at the Seletar Naval Base to the north.

As news of the surrender became known, looters fought each other for merchandise in the well-stocked department stores of Robinsons, Littles and Whiteaways in the heart of the city while other looters broke into the Singapore Cold Storage and Chinese grocery stores along Orchard Road. Soldiers roamed in large groups; some with guns, some in uniform, others in civilian clothes. They jammed Clifford Pier and the waterfront along Beach Road, hoping to hi-jack any vessel to take them to the nearby Riau islands although they might have known their freedom would be brief before they were captured and executed by the Japanese. These tired, despondent troops had withdrawn all the way from Kedah in north Malaya and had finally arrived at 'the point of no retreat' — the Singapore waterfront.

Rotting bodies were on roads, in drains or beneath the ruins of bombed shop-houses and buildings. Nobody was removing the corpses or attending to the wounded in the streets of Chinatown, a favourite target of Japanese bombers and artillery. 'They're bombing Chinatown on purpose because the Japs hate us! They want to kill every Chinese in Singapore!' said a grey-haired Chinese air-raid warden. He cleared his throat noisily and launched a silvery missile from his lips towards a cloudless, blue sky. *Pt-oooi!*

Each Japanese artillery barrage or bombing added to the casualty list that had risen to an estimated one thousand a day. The figure could have been more since nobody was keeping count.

At the General, Tan Tock Seng and Kandang Kerbau hospitals wounded and dying were placed on the floors of wards and along corridors. New casualties lay in long rows at hospital car parks and signs were put up that said: No Cars Allowed! Wounded Only! Nurses and doctors worked around the clock trying to cope with a situation that grew worse by the hour. Hotels and schools became emergency first-aid stations. Private cars were used as ambulances.

Nobody was fighting fires because the Japanese had turned off the water supply from the Gunong Pulai Waterworks in Johore and were now also in control of Singapore's reservoirs.

A deserted Bras Basah Road at sunset: The skeletons of six burnt-out cars and a bus; the bodies of three men and a woman in a nurse's uniform on the playing field in front of St. Joseph's Institution. More bodies were further up the road.

At the Victoria Street-Bras Basah Road junction: Twenty or more mangled bodies, a woman with her arms around two young children.

Near the entrance to the Convent of the Holy Infant Jesus: The remains of an old man in a drain, the bottom half of his body blown away. More bodies beside open air-raid shelters near the Cathedral of the Good Shepherd and the Raffles Girls School.

At the Victoria Street-Stamford Road junction: The burnt bodies of three women and two children. The remains of an ambulance, its doors and roof blown away by the bomb or shell that had hit it; the dead driver still clutching the steering wheel. Bodies beneath the wreckage.

Beach Road: A European police officer on a motorcycle roars past at full speed. (Why the hurry? Didn't he know it was all over?)

Incredibly, the sound of music drifts from the direction of the Raffles Hotel, now a first-aid station and jammed with casualties. The hotel's orchestra plays 'There'll Always Be An England'. A few defiant voices sing.

As night falls, numerous fires cast an eerie, orange glow and long shadows over the battered and strangely silent 'blacked-out' city.

Groups of silent, frightened people suddenly appear

in the semi-darkness; many wounded, their clothes torn and blood-spattered; mothers clutching wide-eyed children. People hurry along streets pock-marked with shell and bomb craters and strewn with the rubble of destroyed buildings. Like everybody else, they are looking for places to hide from the new owners of Singapore. Thousands of refugees from Malaya had told chilling stories of massacres, rapes and tortures by Japanese soldiers.

Chinatown: Someone shouts, *'Jepun lai-lo!'* ('Japanese are coming!' in Chinese). People scatter into foul-smelling drains as a car approaches at high speed, running over corpses on South Bridge Road. It's a false alarm. The car flies a British and a Red Cross flag and flashes by, its horn blaring.

The morning after the surrender:

The Rising Sun flag flutters in a cheery breeze from the flagstaff on Fort Canning Hill where General Percival had his Command Headquarters and from where the Union Jack had proudly flown for one hundred and twenty-three years. Below the hill, in the filthy, deserted streets, hungry stray dogs sniff among the debris, stagnant drains and corpses.

Later that morning:

An old Englishman in khaki shorts and shirt and wearing a sun helmet stands beside his suitcase outside Fullerton Building (now the Fullerton Hotel). He is on his way to the Padang to join other Europeans for the long march to Changi Prison and internment. His jaw drops and he stares in awe as a column of scraggy but jubilant Japanese troops come into view led by a young, stern-faced officer in a grubby uniform and leather riding boots. They burst into a spirited marching song and pause to scream '*Banzai!*' (Long live the Emperor!)

The old man's eyes follow the column of troops as it passes the shuttered Hongkong and Shanghai Bank and GH

Café on Battery Road, where he had lunched with some friends only the day before. And, now, incredibly, he was on his way to become a prisoner of the Japanese. He picks up his suitcase and wanders slowly away.

The Japanese Occupation of Singapore from February 1942 to August 1945 had claimed the lives of thousands of people who were massacred, died from *Kempeitai* torture or from harsh treatment in prisoner-of-war and slave labour camps. Others perished from disease and starvation.

The actual number will never be known.

'Kempeitai' Torture / The 'Double Tenth' Trial

'The *Kempeitai* was a fearsome force with unlimited powers of investigation and arrest that included the highest-ranking Japanese military officers or civilians. Nobody dared question their powers that obviously came from an inner circle of trusted people under Prime Minister Tojo in Tokyo to whom secret reports were sent by their spies such as Col. Tsuji, the man responsible for the Chinese massacre in Singapore'. — Mamoru Shinozaki, author of *My Syonan, My Story*.

During The Singapore Chinese Massacre Trial, when victims had described the methods used by the *Kempeitai* to torture them, a Japanese witness who was in the packed court shouted: 'What the *Kempeitai* did makes me sick and ashamed! The Japanese are a peaceful, cultured and nature-loving people who respected life and beauty!'

Although the *Kempeitai* had already made a notorious reputation for itself by the terror it created in every country in Southeast Asia, few people if any knew or dared ask questions about the organization. All that was known about the *Kempeitai* was that it was a 'special force' with unlimited powers of arrest and interrogation among military and civilians. They were officially the 'Military Police' under the control of the War Ministry in Tokyo headed by the Prime Minister, Gen. Tojo.

They were responsible for the security of civilians and the military in Japan as well as for personnel and the military in territories occupied by the Japanese armed forces. They had the option of appearing in military uniform while on official duty or in civilian clothes (or in disguise) while acting as 'undercover agents'. High-ranking military officers avoided contact with the *Kempeitai* 'untouchables' because they were as open to interrogation and arrest as anybody else.

The *Kempeitai* believed a person suspected of committing a crime had to prove his innocence, but was given no opportunity to do so. A 'confession' by the victim was required and to obtain one, he was tortured. Those arrested did not call on friends or family members to testify to their innocence for fear they would also be arrested and tortured and made to sign 'confessions' implicating themselves and others in crimes they had not committed. Those who had 'confessed' to minor crimes were sentenced to terms in prison. Others were quickly executed.

The Japanese regarded torture as essential when interrogating a person suspected of having committed a crime.

'Light torture' such as beating the victims' naked bodies with canes or ropes, punches, slaps and kicks were used in 'minor' offences. During the interrogation of those suspected of more serious crimes of a political (anti-Japanese) nature, 'heavy torture' was used for which the *Kempeitai*, through years of such experience in China, had become torturers *par excellence*, having perfected methods for causing the maximum pain and suffering of their victims.

The Japanese army, navy and air force each had their own *Kempeitai* investigation teams who were graduates of

Kempeitai Training Schools in Japan and which were operated by the War Ministry. Specialised training was provided to students who had shown the necessary 'aptitude' for administering torture without showing any emotion or sympathy for their victims. Torture for the purpose of obtaining confessions was explained in official manuals and circulated to various military units.

Listed under 'common tortures' were these 'treatments' (translated from the official *Kempeitai* manual in Japanese):

Water Treatment: The victim's hands are tied to his sides. He is made to lie on his back. One end of a rubber hose is attached to a water tap and the other forced down his throat. The water is turned on full until the victim's stomach becomes distended. His stomach is then jumped upon. After this the victim usually losess consciousness. He is revived and the process repeated again.

Burning And The Electric Shock Treatment: 'Live' electric wires are attached to the most sensitive parts of the victim's body. Lighted cigarettes, candles, boiling oil or water are applied to the victim's nostrils, ears, sex organs and in the case of women, also to their breasts.

Knee Spreading And Kneeling On Sharp Edges Treatment: The victim's hands are tied behind his back. A thick, wooden pole is placed behind both knees and an interrogator jumps up and down on the victim's thighs. This results in the victim's knee joints being torn apart. The victim is also made to kneel on sharp edges for very long periods although his kneecaps are broken and bleeding. If he cries out in pain, he is beaten with ropes or canes.

Tearing Out Fingernails And Toenails Treatment: This is done with pliers. As a 'preliminary', toothpicks are inserted under the nails before being torn out.

Breaking Fingers Treatment: Sticks are placed

between the victim's fingers and squeezed, fracturing the bones.

Body Suspension Treatment: The victim's body is suspended by the wrists or neck or hung upside down by the legs. Interrogators then try and pull the victim's joints from their sockets.

Eardrum Piercing Treatment: The sharp ends of pencils are inserted in the victim's ears. The interrogator using the palms of his hands forces the pencils further inwards until they pierced the victim's eardrums.

The *Kempeitai* was established as an 'elite' corps by an order of the Meiji Council of State in January 1881 for the purpose of enforcing discipline among the armed forces. In 1920 it included other more sensitive matters in its sphere of operation with the establishment of the Tokaka or Special Service Unit. The unit which was also known as the 'thought police', paid special attention to political 'thoughts' and pro-communist activity among the armed forces and civilians.

By 1930, the *Kempeitai* had become a force with unlimited powers of arrest and operated with impunity in both the civilian and military sectors. It was used extensively in Japan's overseas colonies, such as Korea and Formosa (Taiwan) to crush 'anti-Japanese elements'.

In 1943 there were 362 *Kempeitai* personnel in Singapore and 758 in Malaya, a small force, comparatively speaking, but one which had many thousands of informers who were mostly Chinese secret society gangsters, waitresses and prostitutes and those of other races with criminal records who were obliged to provide information to save themselves from torture or execution. Many times, as was revealed during War Crimes Trials, the information against people was false because the informers had grudges against them. But, since it was the *Kempeitai's* policy that an arrested person had to prove his innocence (and gave him no opportunity to do so) those accused of false crimes were tortured and even executed.

The *Kempeitai* were everywhere, in their khaki uniforms with white armbands on which were large, red characters meaning *Kempeitai*. Or, they could be disguised as Chinese hawkers, labourers, coffee-shop waiters and trishaw-riders. Many spoke Chinese dialects, Malay and English. Once a person was arrested and was fortunate to be released, the *Kempeitai* made sure that he or she became an informer by threatening them with re-arrest and torture. Each person was forced to recruit at least three informers. In this way, a *Kempeitai* unit in charge of a district had an 'invisible' force a many hundreds of informers.

Each Japanese army division operating in occupied territories in Southeast Asia had a *Kempeitai* unit (known as Field Military Police) attached to it and also to each naval unit. Besides informers, these units were also backed up by civilian police forces. *Kempeitai* units could also call upon troops belonging to the army divisions to which they were attached, for any support in large-scale operations such as the *Sook Ching* operation in Singapore.

Following the surrender of Singapore on 15 February 1942, the first to enter the city was the 9th Infantry Battalion under Maj.-Gen. Saburo Kawamura. It included a special force known as the *Keibeitai* that comprised *Kempeitai* and *Hojo Kempeitai* (Auxiliary Military Police). It is interesting to note that the *Keibeitai* was created on the orders of none other than Col. Masanobu Tsuji, the 'organiser-in-chief' of the Chinese Massacre. Its duty was to make sure security in the city was strictly observed and that the enormous amount of weapons surrendered by the British did not fall into the hands of Chinese guerrillas or other 'anti-Japanese Chinese elements'.

The first *Kempeitai* headquarters in Singapore was at the Tanjong Pagar Police Station under Capt. Haruji Hisamatsu whose unit included several Hokkien-speaking Japanese soldiers.

One of the first things the *Kempeitai* did in Singapore was to order the civilian police to modify every radio, so that no foreign broadcasts from the BBC London or the Voice of America (VOA) could be received and only 'local' broadcasts from 'Radio Syonan'.

The penalty for listening to foreign broadcasts was death. Numerous people who defied the ban were executed or tortured to death, although there were never any reports published in the newspapers of their fate since the *Kempeitai* did not allow anything they did to be made public. However, news of the fate of these victims and others 'taken away' by the *Kempeitai* and held in their separate detention stations (such as the YMCA building in Orchard Road, the Cockpit Hotel in Oxley Rise and a block of converted shop-houses in South Bridge Road) was passed along the 'bamboo telegraph', a secret communication line operated by certain 'anti-Japanese elements', whose identity was never revealed.

The presence of the *Kempeitai* in Singapore was everywhere. Beatings were carried out openly in streets. Suspected 'anti-Japanese elements' were taken away in waiting lorries. Some were released after interrogation and torture while others were not seen again.

The 'Double Tenth' Trial

A description of *Kempeitai* brutality was given by Lt.-Col. Colin Sleeman in his opening address for the prosecution at the 'Double Tenth' Trial (*see Note below*) that opened in

Singapore on 18 March 1947. He said:

'It is with little or no diffidence and misgiving that I approach my description of the facts and events of this case. To give an accurate description of the misdeeds of these men (the Japanese accused) it will be necessary for me to describe actions which plump the very depths of human depravity and degradation. The keynote of the whole of this case can be epitomised by two words: unspeakable horror. Horror, stark and naked, permeates every corner and angle of the case from beginning to end, devoid of relief or palliation. I have searched diligently amongst a vast mass of evidence to discover some redeeming feature, some mitigating factor in the conduct of these men which would elevate the story from the level of pure horror and bestiality, and ennoble it, at least, upon the plane of tragedy. I confess that I have failed.'

> **Note:** The 'Double Tenth' Trial concerned the torture and killing of fifteen civilians interned at Changi Prison, Singapore. They were among a number of internees suspected by the *Kempeitai* of operating shortwave radio transmitters and being in contact with British saboteurs who had secretly arrived in the neighbouring Riau islands from Australia. In a series of raids they blew up Japanese shipping in Singapore harbour. The arrests of internees at Changi Prison were made on 10 October 1944 (the 10th day of the 10th month, hence 'Double Tenth').

Chinese Evacuation

The first signs that the war was beginning to turn against Japan was seen in August 1943, when the Japanese Administration in Singapore launched a 'grow more food' campaign and conceded it was necessary 'because of enemy activity' that was affecting even the scanty food supplies to feed Singapore's population.

In February 1943, after six months of bitter fighting, the Americans drove the Japanese out of Guadalcanal in the Solomon Islands which lie to the north of Australia. The following month a large segment of the Japanese navy was destroyed in the 'Battle of the Bismarck Sea', off New Guinea.

In November, the Americans invaded Bougainville Island off New Guinea as the Japanese were pushed back towards the north. American and British submarines were sinking ships carrying food supplies to Japanese forces in Southeast Asia (including Singapore) and remote islands in the South and Central Pacific. The Japanese confiscated all food produced in occupied territories for consumption by their armed forces and also to build up reserve supplies. This resulted in severe food shortages for civilian populations.

Army strategists in Tokyo, concerned about the Japanese defeats in the Southwest Pacific were also worried about the defence of the territories their forces had occupied in Southeast Asia. They decided it would be a good idea (and would also help towards solving the irritating 'Chinese

Problem') if they used the shortage of food supplies as an excuse to move as many Chinese as possible out of Singapore.

The 7th Area Army which was in charge of the defence of Singapore, was ordered to 'evacuate 300,000 Chinese immediately, to be followed by more evacuations as soon as possible'. The High Command in Tokyo had feared that if the British or Americans decided to invade Singapore, the entire population, especially the Chinese, would give their fullest cooperation to the Allied forces. Thus, the city administration authorities were told to organize the evacuation with military assistance.

Mamoru Shinozaki, who was now Chief Welfare Officer, was ordered to take charge of the entire operation. He later said he had 'a vision of a Chinese settlement safe from persecution by the *Kempeitai*'.

He called a meeting with the Overseas Chinese Association chaired by his old friend, Dr Lm Boon Keng. A committee was appointed to select a site in Malaya where a Chinese settlement could be established.

Land at Endau in northeast Johore was selected. It would have to be cleared of jungle before houses for the settlers could be erected and crops could be planted. A little settlement known as 'New Syonan' resulted with the appearance of food stalls, shops, a paper mill, workshops and a sawmill. The population increased and a branch of the Overseas Chinese Banking Corporation was opened.

A few members of the settlement's committee were shot and killed by guerrillas of the Malayan Peoples Anti-Japanese Army (MPAJA). Shinozaki realised if the killings continued people would begin leaving the settlement. To prevent this, he made a secret agreement with the guerrillas, offering them a supply of rice if they stopped the killing.

The attacks stopped. At the end of the World War II,

12,000 families returned to their homes in Singapore and the Endau settlement was taken over by the MPAJA.

The 'Tiger Of Malaya' Surrenders

Lt.-Gen. Tomoyuki Yamashita who took only seventy days to conquer Malaya and Singapore and was known among his colleagues as the 'Tiger of Malaya', was found guilty of war crimes in the Philippines where he was commander when Japan surrendered in 1945.

He was tried by a US court martial in Manila and executed on 23 February 1946.

The charge against Yamashita was that between 9 October 1944 and September 1945 while he was commander of Japanese forces in the Philippines, he allowed men under his command to commit brutal atrocities against Filipino men, women and children.

Five weeks earlier, when Yamashita had come out of his headquarters in the Baguio mountains in Luzon to sign the terms of surrender, he received a shock. Sitting at the table in Government House with the US military representatives was none other than Lt.-Gen. Arthur E. Percival, who had surrendered Singapore in great humiliation to him on 15 February 1942. Their eyes met briefly and they ignored each other each silent with their own memories of an event that stunned the world.

Yamashita's controversial trial began on 29 October and lasted for about six weeks. During the trial, doubts emerged about the fairness of the proceedings and whether Yamashita had actually 'permitted' atrocities by Japanese troops defending Manila against American forces.

The killings did take place. The question was who did it? While evidence showed that civilians including children had been brutally killed in Manila in February 1945 shortly before the city fell to the Americans, there had been no evidence linking Yamashita's troops with the atrocities. Witnesses said the men who were killing and raping civilians had 'anchor' emblems on their caps. They belonged to the *Tokeitai* (the naval version of the *Kempeitai*) and members of the Japanese Naval Defence Force. But, the prosecution insisted that Yamashita was responsible for the atrocities since an order from Tokyo on 8 January 1945 had also put him in command of 'all naval troops in the Philippines who were engaged in land operations'.

Henry Keys, the correspondent for the London *Daily Express* and who later worked for *The Straits Times*, Singapore, wrote in a despatch from Manila: 'The Military Commission continues to act as though it wasn't bound by any law or rules of evidence...in no British court of law would an accused have received such rough treatment as Yamashita...his American counsel haven't had a hearing!'

Yamashita in his defence had denied all knowledge of the atrocities and went on to say that he had been ordered to take command of Japanese forces in the Philippines only two weeks before the Americans landed. Ironically, the court gave its decision on 7 December 1946, the fourth anniversary of the Japanese attack on Pearl Harbour. Before the verdict was given Yamashita said, 'I swear before my Creator and everything sacred to me that I am innocent of the charges made against me.'

The Commission announced that he was 'guilty as charged' and sentenced him to death by hanging. He shook hands with everybody and began giving away his campaign ribbons, Chinese 'good luck' charms and leather belt. He then calmly walked out of the courtroom.

Unsuccessful appeals against the sentence of death followed. On 8 February the US War Department was advised that President Harry S. Truman would take no action on the petition for clemency. Yamashita received the news calmly. He might have expected such an end because before he left his headquarters in the Baguio mountains to sign the terms of surrender he had told his staff members, 'Once the Americans arrest me, they will never let me go. My only release would be death.'

He then wrote: 'The world I knew is now a shameful place. There will never come a better time for me to die.' When the prison guards came to take him to the gallows on the morning of his execution, he turned towards Tokyo and bowed solemnly and walked with dignity to the scaffold.

It might be argued that Yamashita's trial was one-sided and the 'atmosphere' during his trial was that the Americans were determined to hang him. This attitude was reflected in a remark by Major Kerr, the Chief Prosecutor, when he said he had wished to kill Japanese in battle but if he could hang them instead, it was all the same to him.

But, while Yamashita might have been given the benefit of the doubt when he said he was not aware of the Manila atrocities, it is difficult to imagine that he had no knowledge of The Singapore Chinese Massacre.

The Singapore massacre did not involve the navy but was entirely handled by the army over which Yamashita had overall command. Moreover, the planning of the massacre was organised and supervised by his Chief Operations and Planning Officer, Col. Masanobu Tsuji.

That Yamashita had 'no knowledge' of the Singapore massacre becomes even more difficult to accept since four generals under his command took part in the operation on orders directly from his headquarters, although it may be argued that Col. Tsuji had issued these orders without Yamashita's approval. Even so, Yamashita must have had some knowledge of what was going on at the Chinese registration centres (everybody in Singapore knew!) and that lorry-loads of Chinese civilians were being taken away for execution day and night for two weeks? If this was not what he had wished to happen, why didn't he stop it? Was he totally unaware of the killings and was 'kept in the dark' by Tsuji? Did he realise it would have been useless to have tried to stop Tsuji who had the full support of the all-powerful *Kempeitai*? Was it also because he realised Tsuji went 'over his head' and had received prior approval from Prime Minister Tojo in Tokyo?

Many reasons were advanced for Yamashita's downfall after the surrender of Japan in 1945.

Did he become too popular at home after his sensational victories in Malaya and Singapore that at the same time had made his political enemies envious and wanted his removal? Did Tsuji, whom Yamashita never liked, use his influence with Tojo to bring down Yamashita's popularity? After he had captured Malaya and Singapore, his career appears to have bungled.

Yamashita was commander of the 25th Army until August 1942. Lt.-Gen. Saito took over command in March 1943. Yamashita was recalled to Tokyo and spent some time in China before being sent to the Philippines to deal with a full-scale American invasion early in 1945. He had only two weeks in which to prepare his defence strategy.

There had always been 'bad blood' between Gen. Tojo and Yamashita. When Tojo resigned as prime minister in 1944, he was replaced by Kuniaki Koiso, a retired army general.

Tojo must have been fully aware that Yamashita's troops had no chance whatsoever against superior US forces under Gen. MacArthur.

Did Tojo have something to do with Yamashita's appointment in the Philippines knowing that he would be sending an old enemy and Japan's greatest general to his death in disgrace?

Whatever the issues, Yamashita could not have evaded responsibility for The Singapore Chinese Massacre.

The Japanese Soldier

No record of Japan's sensational military successes in the Pacific War would be complete without mention of a Japanese 'weapon' unlike anything seen before in modern warfare.

The 'weapon' was the fearsome, robot-like Japanese soldier.

He was the 'ideal warrior'. He would fight without food or water and sustain himself on his ability to withstand pain and hardship that he accepted as part of a soldier's duty. He obeyed orders to commit suicide or to carry out suicide attacks without question and was happy to know that he would die like a hero for his Emperor. He was ready to be blown to pieces, shot or horribly wounded. Above all, he welcomed death.

Prime Minister Tojo had made it clear that if a Japanese soldier allowed himself to be taken prisoner, he should be executed even if he escaped and rejoined his regiment. Furthermore, the soldier's family would suffer the shame for his cowardice. (Tojo had tried to commit suicide while in prison in Tokyo during his trial for war crimes before an International Military Tribunal in 1946. He was hanged.)

What puzzled officers and men of the Japanese army was the deep concern of Allied commanders that their troops who had surrendered or were captured would be given 'humane treatment' according to International Law, as laid down at the Geneva Convention at the end of World War I.

Japanese army commanders failed to understand why surrendered Allied troops who were in good health should be treated with special care. To them, it didn't make any sense.

It must be pointed out, however, that the Japanese were not born with the fearsome and fearless qualities that had made them such legendary warriors. The truth is: They were moulded into robot-like 'exterminators' by brutal training methods (that had shocked Western military observers) and in indoctrination courses in which tyrannical instructors instilled in recruits the belief of their 'superiority' as warriors; that through suicidal acts in battle they would reach god-like status, their spirits forever revered at Yasukuni Shrine in Tokyo, the resting place of the spirits of all national heroes.

The Japanese soldier's duty was simply to obey orders. Death was part of it.

Japanese officers were forbidden to take lessons in swordsmanship. The reason, they were told, was because they would have the urge to defend themselves when the whole purpose of fighting was for a soldier not to be concerned about his protection but to die while using every means to kill as many of the enemy as possible.

Defence was negative. Attack was positive. Death was glorious.

The acceptance of the glory of dying in battle was demonstrated by the 'suicide bombers' or *kamikaze* ('Divine Wind') pilots who crashed their bomb-laden planes on to the decks of US warships in the final stages of the Pacific War.

Note: Japanese forces surrendered following the atomic bombings of Hiroshima and Nagasaki in 1945, but only after being ordered to do so by the Emperor. Yet, many 'die-hard' followers of *bushido* (the code of the *bushi* or 'soldier') chose to commit *seppuku* or *hara-kiri* (ritual suicide) rather than face the shame of surrender.

To attempt to understand the 'make-up' of this 'fighting phenomenon' would require going into the origins of the Japanese and the belief that they and the islands they inhabited were created by the gods. They were a 'divine, master race' selected to 'lead the world' under their god, the Emperor.

Only some officers in the Japanese armed forces could claim to belong to the elite *samurai* class. A very large majority were the sons of peasants and the working class. They had heard frightening stories of the brutal methods used by instructors at army training camps to instil the 'fighting spirit' into the hearts and minds of the young recruits, many fresh from school.

When a Japanese soldier informed his parents that he was being sent to war, they also accepted the fact that he was going to die.

The origins of *Shinto*, the national religion, could be traced to ancient times, long before the coming of Buddhism, Confucianism or Taoism. There were three distinct periods to its history:

1. The early period before Buddhism from Korea was introduced in the 6th century AD. 2. The medieval period from the 6th century to the 10th century with the restoration in 1868 of the Imperial Throne. 3. The 'modern' period in which *Shinto* became vital as a medium when demonstrating total loyalty (*kodo*) to the Emperor.

The first period was concerned with primitive 'nature worship' brought about by supernatural beliefs in the objects and forces of the natural environment. From this emerged the ancient shrines and temples of the nature-cult concentrated around a *shintai*, or divine body.

Hero-worship among followers of the cult came later with the Emperor (the direct descendant of the sun-goddess Amaterasu who was 'ruler of the heavens' with her brother Susanowo, the storm-god) as the main symbols of devotion.

The *Shinto* belief includes a story of the Creation of how, from out of the primeval chaos and darkness, there appeared a divine couple named Izanagi (The Male Who Invites) and Izanami (The Female Who Invites) who in turn produced the sacred islands of Japan, the Spirits of Nature and the 'high gods' Amaterasu, Susanowo and the moon-god, Tsuki-yomi.

The second period began with the influence of the non-religious and ethical ideals of Confucianism and the religious philosophy of Buddhism. However, it did not mean that *Shinto* was forgotten. Sacred Shinto records were preserved to maintain ancient traditions and the belief in the divine origins of the Imperial Family.

In time, Buddhism and Confucianism came to be regarded as 'alien beliefs' that had been imported and were not 'pure Japanese'. It led to the acceptance of 'pure *Shinto*' that increased devotion and loyalty for the Emperor and ended the dominance of *shoguns* (feudal warlords). This was the period of *Meiji*, or 'enlightened government' that saw another revival, the belief in the divine lineage of the Emperor and the Imperial Throne. It led to the establishment of 'State *Shinto*', its chauvinistic code of nationalism as well as the *samurai* or 'warrior caste'.

The Emperor Meiji's decree in 1873 ending the feudal era also saw the emergence of a modern Japanese army. The decree contained the famous 'Five Words' or 'principles' to be observed by a soldier. They were: Loyalty; Courtesy (kindness); Courage; Honesty and Contentment (a simple life).

When Japan went to war in 1941, the *samurai* caste had already been abolished in 1868. However, Japanese premier General Hideki Tojo quickly seized the chance to incorporate *samurai* ideals into the *Senjinkun* (Warrior Code) that was taught to officers of the Imperial Army whose harsh treatment of troops under them was a distortion of the original ideals of *bushido* (Way Of The Warrior). Troops were ordered by their officers to make suicidal attacks against enemy forces or fortifications, as had happened in China. In battle, troops were expected to find the quickest way to end their lives to avoid being taken prisoner. Also conveniently erased from the original principles of *bushido* were 'courtesy and kindness'.

No Western army was able to match the Japanese for courage. As General Sir William Slim remarked during the Burma campaign in 1944, 'Everyone talks about fighting to the last man, but only the Japanese actually do it.'

The Horror Of Nanking

Lt.-Gen. Iwane Matsui and Lt.-Gen. Akira Muto were charged before the International Military Tribunal (Far East) in Tokyo in 1947. They were found guilty and hanged for allowing troops under their command to run wild in a six-week orgy of killing, unbelievable cruelty and rape that began in Nanking on 13 December 1937.

Gen. Matsui was commander-in-chief of Japanese forces in Central China from 1937 to 1938. The International Military Tribunal in Tokyo was told that as troops of his 'Central China Expeditionary Force' closed in on Nanking on 12 December 1937 most of the population had fled from the battered and burning city.

The main strength of the Nationalist Army had retreated after bitter fighting but about 50,000 troops were left behind to defend Nanking. Further resistance not being possible, about 30,000 laid down their arms and surrendered. Not in the habit of taking prisoners of war, the Japanese roped these men together and marched them to the banks of the Yangtse River where they were mowed down by machine-gun fire, their bodies carried away by the river.

During the fighting Gen. Matsui's forces had concentrated their attacks on the south gate of the city. Chinese troops who had not succeeded in regrouping elsewhere, abandoned their uniforms and arms and escaped by the north and western gates to an International Safety Zone that had been set up by neutral countries.

Japanese troops swarmed into the city the following day (13 December) and the carnage began. Groups of drunken Japanese soldiers roamed the city. There were numerous rapes in the streets in the presence of the families of the victims, as Japanese troops cheered. The victims and their families were later bayoneted and locked in houses that were set on fire.

A photograph exhibited at the International Military Tribunal in Tokyo showed a group of grinning Japanese soldiers holding up their rifles with the bayonets protruding through the bodies of young Chinese children.

Evidence was also given at the Tribunal by burial societies and welfare organizations that disposed of more than 150,000 corpses, many of which were grossly mutilated and headless. These records did not include the many thousands of bodies incinerated in the numerous fires in the city or those that had been thrown into the Yangtze River.

The streets and walls of buildings and homes in Nanking were splashed with blood. Bodies, with their limbs hacked off and those that had been obscenely mutilated lay everywhere. People were shot on sight. Some were stripped and tied naked to posts and used as targets to test the marksmanship of the soldiers. Points were awarded for hitting certain parts of the victims' bodies.

Rows of houses and office buildings were set on fire. In Taiping Road, which was the shopping centre, every shop was looted and set ablaze within a couple of days At least one-third of the once busy and densely-populated city had been burnt to the ground with only the charred skeletons of some buildings remaining.

The Japanese attempted to justify the mass killing by

saying that many thousands of Chinese soldiers who had abandoned their uniforms were wearing civilian clothes and it was not possible to tell a civilian from a soldier. The answer to the problem was to kill all young males. In this way, more than twenty thousand young men, including schoolboys, were rounded up, marched to the outskirts of the city and either machine-gunned or bayoneted.

Other evidence showed at least 12,000 people of all ages, including children, were shot, bayoneted or beheaded from December 13 to 16 alone.

Gen. Matsui who was on the outskirts of the city was aware of what was taking place.

He arrived in Nanking on 17 December, four days after he had allowed his troops to run riot in the city, by which time more than 170,000 people had been massacred.

He had admitted at his trial that he had been informed of the atrocities before he entered Nanking. Two days after his arrival, he said, the entire commercial district was still ablaze.

Gen. Matsui must have had a guilty conscience for what had happened in Nanking because before he was hanged in Tokyo, he held a religious ceremony in memory of all those who had died in the massacre and sent his apologies to millions of people who had suffered under Japanese military rule.

'The Rising Sun flag is floating high over Nanking...the dawn of the renaissance in the East is on the verge of appearing,' he had once said. Perhaps he was thinking of the Japan's dream of a 'Greater East Asia Co-Prosperity Sphere' with the Emperor as head.

Matsui had retired from the army when he was recalled to active service by the War Ministry in 1937 and appointed commander-in-chief of the Shanghai Expeditionary Force and later, commander of the Central China Expeditionary Force that invaded Nanking.

On his return to Tokyo he was decorated for his 'meritorious services in China'.

The Military Tribunal was also told that in Shanghai, troops under Gen. Matsui's command had committed numerous atrocities. They had terrorised farms, killing the owners and their families besides raping and looting, as they marched from Shanghai to Nanking.

The End

Bibliography

The Knights of Bushido by Lord Russell of Liverpool (Corgi Books, London. 1960)

Four Samurai by Arthur Swinson (Hutchison, London. 1968)

The Reader's Digest Illustrated Story of World War II, (The Reader's Digest Association Inc. New York, 1970)

Sinister Twilight: The Fall of Singapore by Noel Barber (Fontana Books, London. 1970)

In Seventy Days by E.M. Glover (Muller, London. 1946)

Syonan, My Story by M. Shinozaki (Times Books International, Singapore 1975)

War and Memory in Malaysia and Singapore edited by P. Lim Pui Huen and Diana Wong (Institute of Southeast Asian Studies, Singapore 2000).

The Killer They Called A God by Ian Ward (Media Masters, Singapore 1992)

Tha Battlefield Guide: The Fall of Malaya and The Surrender of Singapore by Ian Ward and Ralph Modder (Media Mesters, Singapore 1989)